Additional Praise for *Sea Dog*

The story of Charles Stuppard is nothing short of inspiring. His rise from poverty to commanding the Navy's most advanced warship exemplifies resilience and determination.

Sea Dog offers invaluable leadership lessons, practical advice, and profound insights. Charles has greatly influenced me as a Naval Aviator, Officer, and leader. This book is essential for anyone who wants to lead with purpose, compassion, and integrity.

—LCDR Chris Kapuschansky,
Former US Navy Blue Angel 2022–23 and
Blue Angel #2, in the movie "The Blue Angels",
US Navy F/A-18 Super Hornet Pilot

Captain Charles Stuppard and I have been friends for many years. His reputation as a senior officer and leader in the Navy is noteworthy. He has been recognized as having a "head and shoulders above" capability to lead and motivate his subordinates, especially under stressful circumstances. *Sea Dog* should be guide for aspiring leaders in all walks of life.

—Colonel Tom McNeil, USMC (Ret.),
President & CEO, Founder of MDL Partners

Enroute to commissioning, USS Gonzalez encountered Hurricane Josephine in the middle of the Gulf of Mexico. Charles exuded an aura of competent authority as we weathered the storm. I was there during this scary circumstance. He is a man who weathers storms and knows what he is doing. He is a leader not just for his time—but for all-time.

—John W. Flores,
Author of "Marine Corps Sgt. Freddy Gonzalez",
Former U.S. Coast Guard sailor

Sea Dog is a road map to become an outstanding leader, one who acts with character, empathy and honor. It is a true guide to success and should be in the library of anyone committed to living an extraordinary life. Dr. Stuppard's story reminds me of my personal story, moving from Haiti at age 17 and becoming an attorney, a colonel and a USAF flight surgeon.

—Dr. Rudolph Moise,
CEO of Comprehensive Health Center, Family Physician

Sea Dog

A Seafaring Captain's Lessons in Leadership

Charles L. Stuppard

WILEY

Published by John Wiley & Sons, Inc., Hoboken, New Jersey.
Published simultaneously in Canada.

For general information on our other products and services or for technical support, please contact
our Customer Care Department within the United States at (800) 762-2974, outside the United
States at (317) 572-3993 or fax (317) 572-4002.

Wiley also publishes its books in a variety of electronic formats. Some content that appears in print
may not be available in electronic formats. For more information about Wiley products, visit our web
site at www.wiley.com.

Library of Congress Cataloging-in-Publication Data:

Names: Stuppard, Charles L., author.
Title: Sea dog: a seafaring captain's lessons in leadership / Charles L. Stuppard.
Identifiers: LCCN 2024044832 | ISBN 9781394248247 (hardback) | ISBN
    9781394248261 (ebook) | ISBN 9781394248254 (epub)
Subjects: LCSH: Stuppard, Charles L. –Biography. | Retired military
    personnel–United States–Biography. | Leadership.
Classification: LCC UB443 .S78 2025 | DDC 359.0092 [B]–dc23/eng/20241015
LC record available at https://lccn.loc.gov/2024044832

Cover design: PAUL MCCARTHY
Cover art: © GETTY IMAGES | STEVE WEST

SKY10097992_020625

To my late mother, Grace, (1922–2019) who gave her all,
so we could have it all.

To my wife, Nidda, who provided me with unconditional love
and support. She is the epitome of a Navy spouse.

To the joy of our lives Javier, Maurice, and Charles who gave us
Jace, Korbin, Ezra, and Noah.

Contents

Acknowledgments

I owe a debt of gratitude to many people who gave me freely of their time and energy, and contributed immensely to my success as a person and as a leader. They made me realize that "To Whom Much is Given, Much is Expected."

I begin with my late mother, Gracieuse "Grace" Destra Stuppard, who left her country and her family to forge a future for her children. Without her, this story would not have been possible.

To my wife of forty years, Nidda Luz Melendez, who left Coamo, Puerto Rico, when she was about 3 years old and moved to New Jersey with her family. We met at Cornell University, and she became the rock of my life. She could have gone to Princeton University and I, to Columbia University, and we would have missed each other. Somehow, the path was laid out for us, and here we are. Her unwavering patience was fully tested as I volunteered her to edit my doctoral dissertation.

To my oldest son, Dr. Javier Stuppard, one of the world's top 100 trombonists, whose perseverance and passion for excellence inspire me. I used to take my sons to Bush Garden when they were young.

After Javier's first performance in Switzerland, I asked him how it was? He responded, "Switzerland looks just like Bush Gardens." We both obtained our doctoral degrees within a week apart.

To my middle son, Lieutenant Commander Maurice Valentino Stuppard, who followed my steps in several ways. At my military retirement, he delivered the poem "The Watch" flawlessly and with style. He was flabbergasted when I presented him with my navy sword. He said to me, "Do I keep it?" I responded, "Of course, you now have the watch."

To my youngest son, Charles "Chuckster" Stuppard, the data scientist and mathematician, who was always the smart and quiet one in the family. We would have a "KFC-father-and-son-dinner" for his birthdays, and he would keep the stubs to remind me of the ones we missed. Maurice and I joke as Navy guys that we are the only two in the family not to be a Golden Key Honor Society member. Javier and Charles followed the example of their mom.

To my brothers and sisters who mean the world to me, Nicole and Eddy Michel, Enive and Josué Coicou, Daniel and Marise, Franz and Martine Zambrelli, Serge and Esther Gilles, Alphonse and Yvette, and Lydia and Paul Coicou. They are my rock star family.

To my nephews and nieces Lydie, Thamar, Rachel, Gloria and Sabine, Richard and Elvis, Danno, Ornella and Natalie, Peter and Manny, Tina, Fafi, Christian and Ricky, David, Tatiana and their children.

To my many cousins from my father's side and mother's side. Our Stuppard family is linked to the Charles, Bonhomme, Dalencourt, Poteau, Coicou, Chery, Compas, Boursicault, Dor, Pinard, Dupuy, Bazin, and Monestime families. They are such a joy with which to be.

To my brothers and sisters from Nidda's side: Cheo, Lucy; Felix, Miriam; Manuel, Michelle; Maria; Mamelta; the late Angel, Lisa; the late Tita and Maryland, and their children. Special mention to nephews and nieces Johny and Raisa,

Charlie, Carlos, Lisa and Dereck, Rob and Lisa, Angelica and Jake, Nelson and Kim, David and Felicia, Edward and Jenny, and Wanda and Tony.

To my friends from Juvenat: Serge Vilvar, Rodrigue Valery, Kelly Gaspard, Frerot Dupoux, Ketty Camilien; from Centre D'education Scholaire (C.E.S): Yvon Fleurival, Marcius, Gasner Roche, and Ronet Germain. Best friends from Spring Valley: Lyonel Alexander, and from Fairchild: Roman Woloszyn and Andy Imperiale.

To my mentors who showed me the way; to name a few: Daniel Holloway, Peter A.C. Long, D.C. Curtis, Tony Watson, Sinclair Harris, Chuck Neary, Byung Min Kim, Danny K. Davis, David Swindle, Tom Daniel, Dick Formica, Leon Bury, Ramses Camille, Jeannine Raphael, Frere Mathelier, and Roger Valentin. Special mention to Phil Kellam, Dave Belote, Ray Gromelski, and Paul Hirschbiel who introduced me to local Virginia politics because if good people do not participate in politics, then the nation is liable to be led by those who are not as good, according to Plato.

To my Navy and military friends who are near and dear to many, to name a few: Robert Blondin, Elaine Luria, Monika Washington, David Coggins, Thomas Crimmins, Bob Cooney, Cary Frame, Stewart Wharton, Cynthia Findlater, Bill Crow, the CNIC "Landlords" of Hampton Roads, the 2004-2006 DESRON 2 CO-s, the 2005-2006 SNMG-2 CO-s, my Arleigh Burke (DDG 51), and JEB Little-Creek/Fort Story team.

To my Cornell University friends and classmates who are very dear to me and include David O'Connor, Gregory Nicholls, Jon Poe, Greg Busby, Jamie Hintlian, Jeannette Perez, Simon Krieger, Tina Gourley, and so many others.

To my Alpha Phi Alpha brothers at Alpha Chapter Alumni Association (Cornell), Tau Beta Lambda (Haiti), and New Delta Lambda (Chesapeake, Virginia) who provided me with a vision of hope and higher ideals.

To my L'Haitienne 925 brothers of The Grand Lodge of Washington D.C., whose mission included making me a better man.

A special thanks to my editor, Bruce Wexler, and the professionals at Wiley: Bill Falloon, Susan Cerra, Purvi Patel, Katherine Cording, Lori Zaher, and Meshach Ravitchandran. They took a ten-year work of love that started after I finished my doctoral dissertation and had gotten used to waking up at 5:00 a.m., and turned it into this book.

Introduction

I can imagine no more rewarding a career. And any man who may be asked in this century what he did to make his life worthwhile, I think can respond with a good deal of pride and satisfaction: "I served in the United States Navy."

John F. Kennedy

When I was a kid living amid the turmoil and poverty of Haiti, I could not have imagined myself on the bridge of the USS Arleigh Burke, in command of the lead ship of the most powerful and sophisticated class of ships in the history of naval warfare.

I'm writing this book to help you imagine what is possible, despite whatever obstacles life throws in your way. I'm writing it to help you imagine yourself as a leader, even if you have not yet attained a leadership position.

As a leader, I've spent my career inspiring, motivating, and teaching, and I hope my stories and leadership lessons will inspire, motivate, and teach.

I started writing this book after watching a YouTube program, "Metropole, Le Point," in which one of the guests said that young Haitians were in dire need of positive role models. Though I know other Haitians who have been highly successful, after watching that interview, I thought that I might qualify as a role model. When I met with a group of professional Haitians in New York City and told them about my career, they suggested I share my story in book form.

The more I thought about the book I wanted to write, though, the more I realized it wasn't just for Haitians but for anyone who aspires to lead and succeed – especially anyone who was not raised in privileged circumstances and wants to become a "good" leader. Good is in quotes because I mean it both senses of the term. These leaders are good at their jobs, but they also are good as human beings. I have always strived to be good and do good work, and I believe this striving has contributed greatly to my success and the success of the organizations for which I worked.

Let me give you a snapshot of my career and in so doing, give you a sense of the lessons I hope to communicate.

After arriving in the US at the age of 19 speaking little English, I learned the language of my new country as well as the way things worked here and managed to graduate from Cornell University with a degree in mechanical and aerospace engineering. With that degree, I secured a job designing and testing jets for the US Air Force. From there, I switched military branches and went through the rigorous US naval officer candidate program featured in the movie, *An Officer and a Gentleman*. I spent many years as an officer on naval ships. After a stint working in the Pentagon in the Global War on Terrorism (I was there on 9/11), I rose to become the commanding officer (CO) on the USS Arleigh Burke. I finished my tour in the Mediterranean Sea as commander of US Surface Strike Group 06-1 and captain of the one US warship assigned to NATO's Operation Active Endeavor, preventing terrorism at sea.

I returned to "land," teaching in the Navy's premier leadership school attended by every senior US naval officer going to command, whether of a SEAL team, a nuclear submarine, or the Blue Angels. After this, I went to Kuwait in command of a special US Navy Task Group in support of the 10,000 sailors deployed as individual augmentees (IAs) fighting the Global War on Terrorism in the Middle East. Then, I was chosen to command the first joint Army-Navy base, comprised of 155 tenant commands from cyberspace to special warfare, with a population of 23,000 personnel. I concluded my naval career in the US Naval War College faculty.

Upon leaving a thirty-year career in the Navy, I became a leader in the private sector, first as vice president of the world's #1 architecture and engineering company, AECOM, followed by a position as chief operating officer (COO) of a start-up company in Washington, D.C., and then served as general manager (GM) of a disruptive technology company in Boston, Canopy Defense. I was running my own company, Consulting & Leadership Services (CLS), when the US congresswoman, representing the Second District of Virginia, asked me to serve as her district director. As of this writing, I'm the dean of administration and dean of students at the Joint Forces Staff College at the National Defense University.

The first takeaway from this career snapshot is that I've enjoyed a great diversity of leadership roles. This diversity is important, because it's allowed me to grasp the leadership strategies and tactics that work – and those that don't work – in a wide variety of situations. I've learned, for instance, that the Boy Scouts' motto of "Be Prepared" is as relevant to leaders as to scouts; that it doesn't matter whether you're commanding a ship or a start-up, preparation is a critical factor in whether you succeed.

The second takeaway is that my journey has been improbable, but its improbability is what makes it inspiring to others – or such is my hope. As you'll learn, I started out having to overcome a lot of obstacles – obstacles that were difficult at the time but that also helped me become a creative, resilient leader. As you might anticipate, a Black officer in the Navy speaking in Creole/French-accented English is a distinct minority. I was shocked by the bias I encountered, but it also motivated me to prove myself. People who have smooth sailing into leadership positions can become flummoxed in rough seas; they don't know how to deal with the unexpected ups and downs. I was unusual in that I was one of the few people on my ship who didn't get seasick through a hurricane. I learned how to lead effectively in volatile, unpredictable environments.

Here is a preview of some other lessons I'll impart in these pages:

- Learn to focus on the right things. It is said that what the captain focuses on, the crew will be fixated on. If you become upset by trivial matters, so will your people, and you'll never accomplish major tasks. Recognize what deserves your undivided attention, and your entire team will lend their support.

- Measure your success as a leader by the impact you have on your organization and the people you lead in five to ten years. The litmus test for leaders is what people say about them after they've left their organizations. I left the ships and people who served under me in better shape than when I first encountered them, and that is a leadership legacy not everyone can claim.

- Create an environment where everyone is motivated to join the team fully; to embrace the camaraderie and accomplishment of a team rather than be a team member in name only.

These and many other lessons will be highlighted throughout the book, extrapolated from my experiences at sea and on land.

As proud as I am of my achievements, I write this book with humility and empathy. Above all else, I want to communicate to readers the value of being a good person, no matter how much fame or fortune you accumulate. The best leaders are the best people, and this theme will be threaded throughout my book.

Now, let me take you back in time and introduce you to a young boy growing up in Haiti who, unbeknownst to him, was learning lessons that would serve him well many years into the future.

Chapter 1

Haiti: Learning Lessons That Last a Lifetime

The secret to success is to choose great parents.

David McCullough

Talk to any leaders and they will say that their upbringing had a profound effect on the leaders they became. I was born in Haiti and spent the first nineteen years of my life there, and I was exposed to two very different leadership styles. The country's leaders, Papa Doc Duvalier and his son, Baby Doc, were dictators, and they led through fear and intimidation. My mother and father, as well as other family members and teachers, on the other hand, modeled different leadership traits. Years later as a military officer, I eschewed the stereotypical fear-inducing style in favor of a more compassionate, participative one. As you're about to see, the roots of this style are anchored in Haiti.

My mother, Gracieuse Destra, and father, Maurice Stuppard, grew up in St. Marc, a town thirty miles north of the capital Port-au-Prince. My mother grew up poor and had to quit school at age twelve, but her family's membership in the Lott Carey Baptist Church provided a connection to a US philanthropist, Dr. Sommerville, who helped her obtain a scholarship to Shaw

1

University in Raleigh, North Carolina. My mother told me that she and my father fell in love when they were eight, but their romance didn't begin until he also attended Shaw University on a scholarship.

My father studied divinity, and my mother studied education and nursing. After Shaw, they returned to Haiti and my father began a fifty-plus year career of preaching the gospel. I used to describe my parents' life of service, stating my father took care of their souls and my mother took care of their mind and body. They got married shortly after returning to the island and settled in the Northern part of Haiti, the Artibonites. My father became a Baptist minister and preached the word of God all over Haiti. He was well-known and recognized in Haiti, mostly amongst the poor. I remember hearing him speaking on the radio. In the mid-1960s, he switched to the church of the Nazarene and settled in Port-au-Prince to pastor a church in Carrefour. They would raise nine children: Nicole, Enive, Daniel, Franz, Serge, Charles, Erntz, Alphonse, and Lydia.

A Lot of Faith and a Little Fighting

It was on Wednesday, January 1, 1958, at 6 a.m., that I landed in St. Marc. My mother had a very difficult time with my delivery. Many years later, she related a strange story about something that happened when I was a young child. She said the devil came to her in a dream and asked her for an exchange. The voice told her, "If you give me Charles, I will give you richness and anything else your heart desires." She categorically refused the devil's deal. Even when my mother was elderly, she would remind me that, "The devil wanted you because he knows you have a special mission."

Haiti was a distinctive place in which to grow up, an island beset by poverty and ruled by a dictator. But it was also a place of many friends and family, of a culture that was rich in tradition and pride. I have come to associate all the events of my life in relation to where I lived. I clearly remember living in the house by the river at Carrefour, a suburb of Port-au-Prince. I remember sitting by the glass window and watching Hurricane Flora causing havoc in the neighborhood. I saw coconut trees bending at impossible angles but not breaking. I saw tin roofs flying. The wind whooshed as it rushed by our brick house with its cement roof, and I grasped the power of nature. Then a calm descended with no more wind, and mother said we were in the eye of the hurricane. I did not know hurricane had eyes. I wondered if it could see where it was going. The year was 1963; I was 5 years old.

My father's church would receive shipments of provisions from America called Sinistré. There were several bags of powdered milk, gallons of white cooking grease, and big bags of barley. The Nazarene church also sent tons of previously owned clothing called Kennedy. The bags and carton boxes were clearly labeled "From the People of the United States of America." I thought to myself, "What nice people those Americans must be who would send free food and clothes to people they do not even know."

I started school and the teaching method back then relied heavily on rote memory. The teacher would call on us in front of the class. As required then, I would cross my arms as a symbol of respect and start reciting what I memorized the night before as she held the textbook in front of her, ensuring word-for-word regurgitation. Not knowing the lesson was grounds for severe punishment, which varied from kneeling, to facing the wall standing up, to spanking. Worse was the embarrassment in front of all the pretty girls in the class. It seemed that the girls always knew their lessons, but the guys not so much. Now I realize the girls must have felt absolutely pressured to study rather than endure the torture of embarrassment in front of the guys. This must have been the period when I started to take studying seriously. I memorized world and national events, but at no time did the teacher explain to me why a man named Christopher Columbus had to leave his own country to cause the decimation of a million Tainos in Haiti and the subsequent massive exploitation of African people, with the holy blessing of the Christian church and the tacit approval of a so-called enlightened continent. It just did not make any sense to me then, but I continued to memorize the events, the names, and the places.

Leaders need great memories – there is nothing worse than forgetting the names of people with whom you work or the steps of a strategic plan – and from an early age, I was taught to commit facts to memory.

One day, the school director, Maitre Morel, gathered the entire school and said, "This will be a very important day in human history. America is sending three human beings to the moon. Their intention is to land on the moon and walk on it. We do not know what is waiting for them on the other side, and much is uncertain." He then requested that we all pray for these three American astronauts and led us in singing two songs that I would later sing silently when I would be in the war zone in the Middle East or sailing the world's oceans. We even chose one of these two songs at my mother's funeral, fifty years later. One was the French version of "God Will Take Care of Us." The other song was "Fear Not, I Am with Thee." I sang and prayed as I thought of these brave and fearless American astronauts, with all my heart and all my soul. The year was, of course, 1969 and I was 11 years old. Though I did not yet envision myself in similarly heroic circumstances, the astronauts provided me with a model for when I was commanding a ship rather than a spacecraft.

We were dismissed from school shortly after this heroic flight when the Haitian Coast Guard under Colonel Cayard finally rebelled against Papa Doc Duvalier and took to the sea. I met up with my older brother, Serge, and cousins, Daniel and Carmen, in front of the school and we walked the thirty-minute stretch back home. We could hear the ships' guns responding fort Lamentin's cannon shots. After dropping off our book bags at home, we headed to the top of the mountain at "Morne Téqual" where my paternal uncle, Manno, lived. My cousins, Bob and Marco, with friend, Carlos, were already enjoying the battle! From the hill, I could clearly see three Coast Guard ships. The ships were targeting the national palace, but the bullets kept on missing. The Haitian Army Fort Lamentin, at the entrance of the city, was only a few miles from our mountain top view. We saw the ships turning and pointing their guns toward the fort and delivering a few rounds, which also missed. I found out later in the day that one such bullet landed in the backyard of my friend, Jacques, three houses away from ours. Late afternoon, I went to see the obus, French for cannon ball, which was still on the ground. It was shaped like a three-dimensional, triangular, metallic block rounded at the apex. I thought the bullets once they hit their target would blow up, but apparently, they did not. They were designed to make a big hole in a ship or a building. How in the world were they going to destroy the national palace and cause president Papa Doc to run away?

Though I obviously didn't know then that the battle I'd witnessed would be relevant to my future career, I'd already develop an interest in naval warfare. A few months earlier, I had found a book at my Aunt Anthilde's house about D-day and had read about General Eisenhower and the Allies debarkation at Normandy. That was the very first book I remember reading from cover to cover by myself. It gave me an idea about shore bombardment, and the one I saw that day in Haiti didn't fit the definition! I told my cousin Marco about what I read, how the US Seventh Flotte commanded the vast expanse of the Pacific Ocean and how Admiral Arleigh Burke, the famous Seventh Fleet commodore of Destroyer Squadron 23 "Little Beavers," was creating havoc for the Japanese during World War II in the Pacific. If you had told me then that one day, I would be in command of the Destroyer Arleigh Burke, I would have thought you were nuts.

At the time, naval battles were of secondary importance to battles with other kids. During contentious marble games, I would end up in a fight with a boy named Gary.

Gary was stronger and I would end up losing every fight. One day, I got tired of being beaten up and asked Harry Laventure, a friend of my brothers who was a black belt in karate, to teach me a few moves, and he agreed. My first martial art lesson in Harry's living room was a joy. We started with the front stance, walk forward and back, then middle punch, and then high block and low block. We practiced for an hour. In the next lesson, we progressed to front kick and side kick, my favorite. It was a most precious gift from Harry, which he gave to me freely, and I was grateful. One day after a marble game, Gary charged toward me. I stretched into a Shuto Khan stance, wrapped my hands around his waist, and down he went. I could not believe my eyes; my very first victory. My self-confidence soared, and Gary never picked a fight with me again.

My Mother Leaves and a New School Starts

On April 1, 1971, my mother told me she was going to New York. I knew what happened to parents who went overseas: They disappeared and never came back. Later, they sent for their children and family, then abandoned the country. I had lost several friends, like Doddy Mathelier and Ralph Gousse, through these overseas departures, and I remember the circumstances and sadness of each exit. Now, I was losing my mother, the person to whom I was closest. I felt desperate and devastated. I wondered what would happen and how long would it be before I saw her again. We took her to the airport, and she went to the Pan American Airways counter for her ticket. She had on a beautiful dark navy-blue skirt and a matching top over a white shirt – she was always pretty, and she looked especially now as she gave us a final kiss. I could see the tears on her face as we said our goodbyes. She made her way toward the gate, and we all went upstairs to the second-floor open balcony to see her walking toward the Pan American Airways stairway and ascending, as if she were taking a transport to heaven. I did not even wave to my mother; I didn't want to attract the attention of my stern and disciplined father. My eyes instead tracked her every step until she disappeared behind the airplane door. We watched as the airplane lifted into the sky, which was the first time I had seen anything like it. My father had been to the United States several times to preach, but I was never invited to go to the airport with him. I asked my father, "What happens, if as the airplane takes off, it loses air? Can it just fall out of the sky?" I wanted to know if there was a possibility that my mother could be in danger. My father turned toward me and said sternly, "Son, ask God for forgiveness right now! Do not think such bad thoughts." I felt so small and stupid, because he must have thought that it was a wish. I only wanted to know if that was a possibility though, because the most precious love of my life was up there, in that thing. Years later when I was at Cornell University and taking fluid mechanics and studying the effects of turbulent flow on an airfoil, I discovered the answer was yes. It is possible for an airplane to lose altitude, not air as I thought, and literally fall from the sky.

Having passed a rigorous test, I was able to move on in my schooling and registered to attend the best school in our town at Carrefour. Prior to joining that school, I had usually been the top student in my class since kindergarten, with results published monthly and announced publicly. The competition at this new school was tough, and I had to quickly get used to not being number one anymore.

Juvenat Sacred-Heart High School was the place where I began to develop intellectually and spiritually and met some of the best friends of my life. But it was also a place of strict discipline – I learned that it can be carried to negative extremes. You did not want to be called out by the headmaster, Frère Mathelier. One day we were all lined up prior to entering the classroom when I realized we had a test, and I had forgotten my pencil. While in line, I asked a fellow classmate to borrow one. From the second floor where he addressed the entire school daily, Frère Mathelier saw me talking and immediately called, "Stuppard, report to my office." After he was done talking, each class filed to their classroom, starting with the most senior class. I patiently waited for my class to file in and instead of going to class, I peeled off to the principal's office. There was no discussion, no explanation, he said, "You are not supposed to talk in line, it will cost you." I extended my right palm out and he smacked it with a piece of flat rubber we sarcastically called Ovaltine (i.e. medication for the soul). Then I held out my left palm, and bam, another smack, then right, left, until I got my six. Tears flowed, but I refused to cry – I didn't make a sound. Embarrassed, I went back to class to finish the day.

We learned many lessons – both in academic subjects and in our religious instruction – but some of the learning was unexpected. I had a geology teacher, for instance, who taught us about love. It was Valentine's Day, and he decided to dispense with his usual lesson about rocks in favor of advice about a less tangible subject. He spoke to us about the 3 Cs: Coeur, Cerveau, Corps, which is French for Heart, Head, Health. He explained each one:

> Coeur: when you choose a partner, ensure that he or she has a good heart. What I mean by that is that the person must be kind and understanding. If you are going to spend the rest of your life with a person, you want to make sure that he or she has respect for you and respect for the other people you love, such as your parents. The person needs to be understanding, because you will make mistakes at times. The person needs to be able to help cope with the problems that life brings to all of us, humans.
>
> Cerveau: you want to ensure you go out with someone with a bit of brain. There are some stupid people out there, that you might want to leave for somebody else. If you have a choice and you do, it is at the beginning of the relationship. During the courting period, you each have a chance to assess each other like peacocks. Ensure you have criteria like how they handle discussing topics of interest to you. Does the person care about your issues or do they only talk about themselves trying to impress you? How reliable is that person? Can you depend on them, in times of crisis or during an emergency? These are all questions one should at least think about when we are about to commit to a relationship.

Corps: ensure the person is healthy and compatible. When you wake up in the morning, are you okay with the other person next to you au naturel, with no make-up. Everyone is beautiful in their own way, but let's be true to ourselves; there are some ugly people out there as well, whether spiritually, morally or physically. If you want to choose an ugly person as partner, let it be a conscious decision.

These were valuable teachings, ones I have taught to my children and apply to this day. At the time, though, there was an even higher-level lesson that I took away from this geology teacher's talk about: *Some of the best advice can come from the most unexpected places.*

Struggle and Strife

After my mother's departure, life continued to go downhill for us. One day the water stopped flowing out of the faucet, and it might have been cut because my father did not pay the water bill. We needed water to drink and to bathe. My aunt, Anthilde, and her husband, Beaujour, had water, and they also had food since Uncle Beaujour was working. My cousin, Daniel Poteau, my little brother, Alphonse, and I would go at night to their faucet to fill up a small container, which we would put under our bed or somewhere safe for our own use.

A few months after my mother left, we could not afford the rent anymore. My old teacher's (Jeanine) school was disestablished, and she was using the two-room school structure for storage. My dad asked her to let us use it and we managed to cram our whole family into the two-room former schoolhouse. Sleeping was challenging as we all slept sideways packed like sardines.

This time was probably the lowest point in my life and that of our family. I would walk to school every day, a thirty-minute fast-paced walk. I would never miss a class. My breakfast, when available, usually consisted of coffee and a piece of bread smaller than the palm of my hand. I remember my cousin, Touyoune, and I would sometimes scout the yard for edible grass named croupier that we would boil in a discarded tin milk container. We would make a fire, boil the grass, and give one piece of the roots to my little brother, Alphonse, and to my little sister, Lydia, and then, take some for ourselves, and call it a day – that would be our dinner. One thing for sure was certain, we could be hungry, but we would never go to any neighbor or anyone to ask for food or money. Most Haitians possess a deep pride about who we are and are thankful for what little we have. Most of all, we're proud descendants of the great ancestors who gave us our freedom. We would go hungry and thirsty, as long as we were free in our very own land. At lunch time in school, some of my friends were better off than I and had sandwiches, but I would never tell anyone that I did not have any lunch for the day.

Despite being poor, I remained proud of who I was. I saw the Sidney Poitier movie, *Guess Who's Coming to Dinner*. When I was told it was about racial discrimination, I knew exactly what that meant, despite my young age: some White people believing that they were superior to Blacks, and their respective behaviors and actions toward Blacks. I also understood that many Americans, mostly the White ones, perceived Blacks as a single, undifferentiated group. It was as if I thought of all Whites as the same – Australians, Americans, and Europeans. But I knew this was wrong. I did, however, believe that all Americans were Americans – a false generalization that I corrected years later. The traits I attributed to Americans derived from my limited interaction with them in Haiti. Most Americans I saw were White, kind, and believed in God. Mrs. Moorhead was a Black American missionary who came from Virginia to help with an orphanage not too far from our house. Her skin color was like mine, she spoke English, and had money. I had always assumed that all Americans were rich and had money. It was said then that even the poorest of Americans were better off than a rich Haitian. Mrs. Moorhead looked like my mother, and she had a deep Southern accent; she was as lovely and nice as all other Americans I had met.

This was around the time when I became interested in girls. One day, I mustered enough courage to go and talk to an attractive classmate. I saw her in the hallway coming my way, and I was conscious that she wore much nicer clothes than me – my shoes were torn and tattered. As I approached her, she looked at me with disdain, giving me a dismissive glance. I felt so small at that moment, as if I were trying to reach something beyond my grasp. She was from a higher social class and brushed me off like a bothersome fly. From that moment on, I would empathize with those less fortunate, regardless of my own position.

Father Figures

My father had a violin, but I had never seen him play it. One day, I mustered enough courage to talk to him about it. I was so afraid of him, but my desire to know about the violin was so great that I was compelled to ask. Of course, I had rehearsed every word of what I wanted to request. I approached him and said, "Father, I have something to tell you." He said nothing, merely staring. I said, "Dad, you have a violin. Can you teach me how to play some day?"

To my surprise, he said, "I always knew that this day would come when you would ask me that question. Back when we lived in Duvalier Ville, I played the violin once, and you were probably 3 or 4 years old. You pulled up a chair and sat down, right next to me. You did not say anything, you just sat and listened the whole time I was playing with a quizzical look. I knew that one day you would also play the violin."

My father added that he had a cousin, Maitre Valentin, who taught violin at the Central School, and he also played in the Haitian symphonic orchestra. He told me to go to the school, ask for Maitre Roger Valentin, and explain that I was the son of

Maurice Stuppard and wanted to take violin lessons. Even better, he granted me permission to take his violin to practice. I was happy; this was the first time my father and I had an actual conversation, though he did most of the talking after my request.

I journeyed to the Central school and asked at the front desk where I could find Maitre Valentin, and they gave me directions. When I entered his classroom, I introduced myself as the son of his cousin, Maurice, and said I was there for violin lessons. That was the beginning of a beautiful friendship. He started me with the first lesson and gave me homework. I would go once or twice a week, and though I found the violin to be a difficult instrument, I persevered.

Around this time, my father left his Nazarene church and became associated with a downtown church. One day, he took us to a church service with him. It was a revelation. I was finally old enough to appreciate his qualities as a preacher. He spoke with passion and knowledge, displaying his comprehension of the bible and his fervent belief. When he prayed, it was as if he was talking to God Himself. For him, God was not an entity in heaven but there with him, ever-present and within. He believed he had a special mission in Haiti. Watching him, I realized why he was so often absent from our house – he was fulfilling that mission. He also preached on the radio. I had friends who asked me if Pasteur Maurice Stuppard on the radio was related to me, I replied proudly, "Yes, that's my dad."

One Sunday evening, my father was having a special church service. We always knew that my dad was on the blacklist, first of Papa Doc and then Baby Doc Duvalier, for teaching people about justice, freedom, and other democratic values absent in a dictatorship. For several years, the Duvalier secret police force Tonton Macoutes watched our house, but our dad was never afraid. That Sunday evening, though, they did more than watch. Tonton Macoutes encircled the house, arrested our father, and took him to jail, right in front of us children. Our father spent forty days in prison and my sister, Nicole, brought him meals every day.

When released, our father would join our mother in the US, never to return to Haiti. We moved to our Aunt Luce Bonhomme's house.

Learning in and Out of School

When school started in September 1974, I attended the Center for Education Scholaire (CES), a small private school not too far from the Sacred Heart church at Bois Vernat, which was an influential and nice neighborhood in Port-au-Prince. The houses were beautiful, and most people in the area had nice European cars. Every month, students took scholastic tests in every subject. Test results were compiled with grades tallied from homework and quizzes. Each student was ranked according to their overall score for the month. During the first week of October, the September result came out. The principal stood in front of every class and called out the names of every student and their numerical standing. We had about twenty students in our class. Once you heard your name, you were to walk to the front and get your carnet (i.e. report card) to take to your parents for signature, acknowledging your performance in school. I did not really know what to expect. I was the new kid in town and most of the students had been together since 6eme (sixth grade) and knew each other. They already had their established reputation and pecking order. A new student usually would start at the bottom or perhaps in the middle. Good students normally stay in their schools and do not transfer. Professeur Camille, director of the school, started to speak, "The number one student for this class for this month is ... Charles Lionel Stuppard!" I made my way to the front of the class as a new student that nobody knew. I walked up, shook the principal's hand, and walked back to my seat. People were puzzled; I had displaced the number one guy, Yvon Fleurival. Next month, the same result. At the end of the year for the big exam, I was still number one.

In a way, this was my first leadership position. I had worked hard to attain my rank. My achievement was partly the result of ability. But ability alone is not enough. You had to do the work.

Others might have better connections, be richer, or possess greater intelligence. But often, the most success went to the hardest worker.

Around this time, I discovered another truth: future leaders need mentors. We were offered a First Aid class given by the Red Cross of Haiti, and two instructors came to the school to teach that course. One younger instructor and the number-two leader of the Red Cross was Maitre Leon Bury. He was a gentleman of the highest caliber, like those you only read about in books. He became my very first life mentor. He was the first adult to invite me to his house. He lived two streets away from ours in a very nice house with a fenced area, and we developed a great friendship. I saw him as a mentor, and he treated me like a son. We discussed philosophy and the works that impressed me were "La Bouteille à la Mer" and "La Mort du Loup" by Alfred de Vigny, an eighteenth-century French philosopher. Maitre Bury gave me freely of his time. Back then, I did not have access to the Discovery or the Disney channels. I realized there was so much to learn outside of school, so much wisdom to attain, and I only had an hour or so at a time when I visited with Maitre Leon Bury. I wished I had the books to read, so I could learn all these things he told me. Still, he broadened my thinking, providing me with perspectives that I would not otherwise have had if I confined my learning to school.

The other person who had a great influence in my early life was Maitre Roger Valentin, my violin teacher. I continued with my violin lessons, once a week, on Friday afternoons. At times, he would be busy and had his son, Phillipe, practice with me. I never became very good at the violin, because I did not have the sheet music to practice. It is also not an instrument I could fiddle with like the guitar or the accordion. Once, I was able to attend the national conservatory, Pro-Musica. That was my first and only chance to see Maitre Valentin performing for a live audience. He sounded wonderful. One Friday afternoon, I walked to Maitre Valentin's house to take lessons, and it was raining. He called a taxi and gave me the money to pay for it. I took private violin lessons with him for four years and never once paid him a dime, and he never once asked for anything. He was my hero; he was made of the material of which great men are created. I wanted to grow up to be as kind and as talented as he was. More than anything else, he showed me that a great man doesn't have to be arrogant or harsh; that high achievement and human decency aren't mutually exclusive.

At school, Maitre Ramses Camille taught French Literature. Every weekend, he gave us an essay to write which was due on Monday. The paper had to include a proper introduction, a full development of the subject, and a logical conclusion. He was teaching us to think logically. We had to fully research the topic first, and then write about it. One memorable essay was to compare and contrast Pierre Corneille with Jean Racine in the famous dissertation: "On Dit Que Racine Paint Les Hommes Comme Ils Sont Et Corneille Comme Ils Devraient être. Qu'en Pensez Vous?" Translated as, "They Say that Racine Describes Humankind the Way They Are, and Corneille the Way They Should Have Been. What Do You Think?"

This is a dilemma that leaders face; the real versus the ideal. Though I didn't know it at the time, contemplating this dilemma was excellent preparation for the situations I would face in the Navy.

I also learned another lesson that would prepare me for my leadership roles. I was taking a course in spatial geometry. The professor was trying to explain an esoteric concept of lines in space by drawing them on the blackboard. At a certain point, he lost me. I could not visualize, nor understand, how he came up with his conclusions. I raised my hand and asked a simple question, "Pourquoi?" (why?) He stopped and looked at me. Clearly puzzled and astonished, he said, "In all the years I have been teaching, never once has a student asked me why certain things work while others do not."

As I would discover years later, it's important to follow orders in the military; but it's also important to question why, even when you're obeying commands.

I prepared to take my final state exam, the one that allowed you to go to university, either medical or law school. I often studied to midnight, memorizing innumerable dates, places, battles, and so on. The day of the test arrived, and then we waited weeks for the results, which were announced on live radio. I passed and soon my mother made plans for me and my siblings to join her in the US.

We went to the American Consular Office to obtain our visas, and I'll never forget what the official there said to us: "This is the future of the country leaving the country."

Chapter 2

A Strange New World

When I arrived in the US on August 17, 1977, all I had were the clothes on my back, a hand-tailored suit made by a friend of ours, $14 cash, my father's violin, and two books: one about Freemasonry, a gift from my friend, Vanel Jean-Francois, and the other was about a US Naval Academy. My brother, Franz, had ordered it, and I was keeping it for him. At the time, I knew nothing about the Navy, and I didn't dream about joining.

On the plane, I sat by the window so I could see outside, as it was my first time ever inside an airplane. (Little did I know that only seven years later in 1985, I would be in the cockpit of a T-2 Buckeye Jet aircraft talking to air traffic controllers as a US Naval aviation student.) To see clouds and be in the clouds was a wonder; I was fascinated. The entire trip into the unknown was like a dream. After three hours of flying, we arrived at John F. Kennedy International Airport (JFK).

Over the years, I have learned the skill of adaptation – making smooth transitions to different environments, people, and challenges. This is an essential leadership skill, and I began learning it when I arrived in this new country. If a place could be any different than Haiti, the journey from JFK to upstate New York was it.

How can there be so many cars on one road at the same time and all going so fast? I was fascinated by the many streetlights, the way the highways were lit with their reflection on the roads, and the wonders of technology at work. I was just soaking it in; it felt like being on another planet. Then we left the city lights, passed the George Washington Bridge, and made a right turn onto the Palisades Parkway. I just could not believe my eyes as I saw the double level of the George Washington Bridge. How can one bridge support so much weight? What kind of people were so smart to build giant bridges like that?

We arrived in Rockland County, where my family lived in an apartment building. Though I could understand some English, people spoke it way too fast for my brain to comprehend easily. Still, I was surrounded by friends and family from Haiti, making the transition a bit smoother.

Working to Earn, Learning to Work

My priority was to enroll in Rockland Community College, but I also needed to get a job and make money. Uncle Bill Villardouin, the husband of my mother's cousin, Aunt Elza, had a cleaning business. A week after my arrival, my mother asked him for a job for me, and he said he had something. I needed to meet him at 4:00 a.m. in Cinema 45 on Route 45, in Spring Valley. My mother walked the three miles with me, we knocked at the cinema door, and Bill opened it for us. He showed me how to clean the movie theater, starting with sweeping all the popcorn from each aisle to the main hallway, and then picking it up. Then I watched him clean the bathrooms. He cleaned everything, and in two hours, turned that messy place, full of popcorn and syrup on the floor, into a beautiful movie theater.

He offered $5 an hour and added that the job takes two hours; I would make $10 a day. My weekly $70 wages paid for gas, car insurance, college lunches, and martial arts classes. For the next three years, I worked every day, including Christmas Eve, Christmas day, New Year's Eve, and my birthday, which is New Year's Day; I never missed a workday. I threw myself into the job as if it were the most important one in the world. I have always had a strong work ethic; doing the best job possible, and always showing up are simple are exceedingly effective ways to succeed.

During this time, I began going to classes at Rockland Community College. I took an English class because I needed to improve my vocabulary, my pronunciation, and my listening skills. My professor, a White woman, was outstanding. She was my first close contact with a White person. She took her time to teach me personally and accept me for who I was. Unlike in Haiti, I did not have to listen to her or anyone else preach or sing as part of school.

I took many different courses, including organic chemistry, in which I received an A, and American history, which was harder because the teacher spoke too fast. As part of my physical education requirement, I signed up for yoga. I had studied Hatha Yoga in Haiti using a book that I'd borrowed. I discovered the philosophy of yoga, not just the exercises, learning about chakras. In that class, I met Allen, who was my very first White friend; he was also Jewish. He did not care that I was Haitian. For him, I was just another student.

When I was at Sears shopping center in Monsey, NY, I saw an ad for Taekwondo martial arts classes and met with Korean Grand Master Byung Min Kim. I began taking classes shortly thereafter. Though I had learned some martial arts in Haiti to defend myself against bullies, this was a different level. I practiced everyday Monday through Friday. I went to adult class from 6:00 p.m. to 7:00 p.m., and most nights would stay for the 7:00 p.m. to 8:00 p.m. class as well. Taekwondo became my passion. My entire life revolved between going to school, studying and doing homework, and cleaning the movie theater after the last show at 10:00 p.m. or early morning before going to school. For my black belt test, I had to do the forms, break several boards, and fight several students as well as other black belts. I passed and was given my black belt. I could do a flying side kick to break boards over ten people laying on the floor side to side. I could jump between the heads of two people standing back-to-back with their heads slightly leaning forward and then break a few boards.

In Taekwondo, Master Kim taught me to focus on the actual movement I was performing. In my mind's eye, I must also see how the movement was supposed to be performed. A picture of the ideal in my mind must be present; I needed to know what the perfect move looked like. I could only envision the move if I had seen it performed. Fortunately, Master Kim's form was the ideal. Each movement had to be performed with perfection.

Focus and concentration helped me. Focus was the direction the mind was looking into; concentration represented the time factor – how long the mind keeps on looking in that direction. I needed to focus on every move and concentrate the entire form until full completion.

Leaders need to be able to focus and concentrate, especially in times of confusion and chaos. Though there are many ways to acquire these skills, martial arts was the method for me.

It paid dividends early on, especially in my education. When I was in class, I tried to focus on what the professor was saying and not day dream. I visualized the teacher being there for me and me alone. That professor was spending all his energy on me and he existed at that moment to carry a conversation with me. Shame on me if I did not respond to the conversation. Focus and concentration helped me to be disciplined.

I had a unique opportunity that was not to be wasted. I understood the sacrifice of my mother. I understood the sacrifice of all those who came before me. My grandparents and ancestors did not have the same opportunity. They had to fight hard to win the right for me to sit where I was and to learn.

I learned not only in the classroom and in martial arts training, but outside of these venues. I was especially aware of what it meant to be Black in the US. In my interaction with Americans in Haiti, it was mostly with White Americans because of the church. There were few Black Americans. I did not know there existed two different Americans within America, a White America and a Black America. I realized that my new country had many foreigners who became Americans. When French, Japanese, or Russians became US citizens, they immediately joined the White American crowd. When Jamaicans, Kenyans, or Haitians became US citizens, they instantly became Black Americans (or African Americans). I would learn much more about what it meant to be Black in America in the years ahead.

Cornell: An Educational Dream

My brother, Franz, was determined that I should apply to Cornell University as I was finishing my second year at Rockland Community College. When I started reading about Cornell University, I discovered that the probability of me attending this institution was as good as me becoming an astronaut. Not only was Cornell University among the most selective of colleges, but the tuition cost was exorbitant. Nonetheless, I applied to attend starting the Fall of 1979, and shortly thereafter, Cornell University rejected me.

Undeterred, I tried again the following year, applying not only to Cornell University but also Columbia University and many other schools. I ended up being accepted to Columbia University first, and then the Cornell University letter arrived; I was accepted! I'd visited Cornell University with Franz and other family members and had fallen in love with the beauty of the campus. As enthusiastic as I was about the engineering program at Columbia University, Cornell University offered me a better financial aid package, so that's where I decided to go (missing out on the opportunity to meet another aspiring Black student at Columbia named Barack Obama).

When I arrived at Cornell University for the fall semester, I could hardly believe that I was a student there. I remember

walking past the Dickson Courtyard, through Balsh Hall and out
to the big yard in front of Balsh Hall, overlooking the main campus. I walked to the main campus and crossed the Cayuga River
using the famous suspension bridge. I continued to admire the
campus as I passed the Uris Graduate Library on my left and Olin
Undergraduate Library on my right. I stopped in Olin, and I was
floored by the paintings and numerous books. I thought, "How do
I read all these books?" I finally made it to the Engineering Quad
containing ten buildings, each dedicated to a field of study, including the Mechanical and Aerospace program.

I registered for my classes and was all set to start the first semester.
I realized how fortunate I was. I walked to my room, got on my knees
and praised God, offering thanks and glory for answering my prayers.

I attended Cornell University during Professor Carl Sagan's
Cosmos: A Personal Voyage TV series. This world-famous professor
worked and taught on campus and was available to me and every
other student any time. We also had other famous professors such
as Nobel Prize winner for physics, Hans Bethe, and various others
in several fields. It was a place of great intellectual stimulation and
stress, and I reduced the latter by playing intramural soccer and
teaching Taekwondo.

*Again, the discipline of martial arts served me well in the classroom. I
discovered that I was capable of bringing great intensity to challenging
problems, able to spend hours wrestling with difficult problems – an ability that would prove useful years later when dealing with issues of enormous complexity.*

I will never forget attempting to solve a fluid mechanics problem. I sat on my chair behind my desk on the fifth floor of Dickson
Hall and watched the sun setting at about 6:00 p.m. I kept working
on it all night and behold, by 5:00 a.m., the sun came back up, and
I was still behind the desk working on the very same problem. By
6:00 a.m., eureka! I had solved it. The homework was due at
8:00 a.m., giving me two choices: Stay awake, go to breakfast and

then to class, or ditch breakfast, take a quick nap, and set the alarm clock for 7:30 a.m. I decided to do the latter and went to bed. I missed the alarm and woke up at 7:50 a.m. I jumped out of bed, got dressed quickly, and ran to class. When I got there, class was about to start. I turned in my homework and sat down. The professor was talking about the Navier-Stokes equation, and I was following his every word as he wrote several equations on the board describing partial factors like DX/DT, DY/DT, DZ/DT, and DV/DT in a three-dimensional matrix as the flow was being affected by some force and reacting to that applied force. I was there in the flow, so caught up in the behavior of the fluid in a non-laminar flow pattern that I closed my eyes, listening to Professor Warhaft's beautiful British accent. Then suddenly for an unknown reason, he stopped talking. I opened my eyes to inquire why. To my very surprise, the classroom was completely empty. Class was over, and everyone had packed their bags then left as I was in the soundest and deepest sleep.

I found that I was intellectually omnivorous. I wanted to consume the world of knowledge one subject at a time. Most leaders are learners, and my learning picked up steam at Cornell University. One of my favorite places was the Uris Library rare books section. Those books, down there in the temperature-controlled basement, were older than dirt. I would go down there to read sections of certain rare books, and soon two or three hours would pass; precious hours that I could have spent studying engineering. I knew the path I had chosen was through science, technology, engineering, and mathematics, but I was also fascinated by philosophy, history, politics, and literature.

Thinking about possible careers, I took as an elective, Nuclear Engineering, an introductory course in atomic energy. I enjoyed that class, gaining an understanding of the challenges faced by Enrico Fermi and Oppenheimer. I received a good grade and the Nuclear Engineering Department offered me a spot to matriculate as a nuclear engineering student, which I declined. I was more interested in airplanes and flight dynamics.

Before the semester ended, I went to Student Placement and completed an application for the Engineering Summer Internship Program. I was accepted to work at Kodak Park Research and Industrial Center in Rochester, NY. That summer at Kodak opened my eyes about how a large organization could still care deeply about its employees. Kodak was very family-oriented and took great care of its people. For the company, it was more than a workplace, it was a family place. It reminded me of a few articles I read about the Japanese way of running business, making people an integral part of the organization.

When I returned to Cornell University for the fall semester, I lived on a coed floor, and my neighbor, Janet, introduced me to her friend, Nidda, who was from New Jersey. One day, the dorm was having a party, and everyone had to bring a date. I asked Nidda if she would come with me, and she said yes. We had a grand time talking and dancing. We got to know each other better and became friends. The friendship developed into a romantic relationship, and we started seeing more of each other.

I enjoyed Nidda's company and used to spend hours just talking to her. I talked a lot about Haiti and its history, and she listened attentively. At times I wondered if I was making any sense to her, but it turned out that she was a brilliant listener who came to understand me at least as well as I understood myself. When I played intramural soccer for the dorm against other groups, Nidda would come and watch the entire game. One afternoon, I remember it was raining and there was only one spectator under an umbrella – it was Nidda.

I'm not giving anything away when I write that before too long, I knew that Nidda was the one.

Honoring Tradition

Many years later as a leader, I found tremendous value in tradition, and I can trace this value back to Cornell University. Some traditions at Cornell University were passed down from one generation to the next. For instance: the ringing of the bells and the beautiful chimes on top of the Olin Library. At certain hours, one can hear the chimes play the Cornell Songs, the Alma Mater Song, "Far above Cayuga Waters."

In the center of campus, you'd come across Willard Straight Hall, the student union building. It was located next to the famous Cornell Tower and across from the library. It was said that all Cornellians were bound to go by there for one reason or another. It was there that the tradition of "face time" would be observed. Hanging out in front of the building, one would see everybody and would be seen by everyone – we referred to this experience as "face time," since it was the time to show your face or see other people's faces. Everyone in our era knew about "face time," and I was surprised when I returned to campus years later and discovered that a new generation had no idea what "face time" meant. I assumed the tradition would be passed down to successive generations. Then I realized the beauty of Cornell's traditions – each class, each group, each fraternity, each sorority, each sports team would have their own traditions. Some of the traditions would disappear, while others would continue with the arrival of new students. Traditions went through a cycle of birth, renewal, death, and rebirth.

In the US Navy, in business, and in government, I learned to respect traditions – to honor some, to update others, and to reject ones that no longer worked. These traditions helped young people, especially, grow and transform, much as they helped Cornell students enter the school with doubt and uncertainty and leave with confidence, ready to take on the world.

Cornell University was where I fully immersed myself in the American culture and way of life – it was where I became an American. And it was where I started to become a leader.

In the fall of 1981, I was an orientation counselor, providing guidance to incoming freshmen and transfer students. I also became more involved in my hall's Living Learning Center, becoming a member of the selection committee that chose the future residents of the hall. These were small leadership roles, but they provided a taste of what leadership was like.

The First Step on a Winding Career Path

I began interviewing with companies that fall. During the year, I interviewed with Schlumberger, Kodak, Xerox, General Dynamics, Bell Helicopter, Fairchild Republic Corporation, and various others. I also thought about applying for graduate school at Stanford University, MIT, Harvard University, and even considered Cambridge University, Oxford University, Sorbonne University, and Heidelberg University. I eventually received job offers from Xerox and Fairchild Republic. I really liked the aerospace field. Back then, the aerospace business was booming with NASA, the space shuttle, the space station, and military jet fighters. During additional interviews with Fairchild, they showed me their production lines and the A/10A aircraft. I interviewed with the head of the landing gear department and with research and development. I received the letter offering me a job as a design engineer to start upon graduation next winter.

My son, Javier Antonio, was born in November 1982, a month before I graduated from the Cornell University School of Mechanical and Aerospace Engineering in December 1982. Immediately after graduation, I took a trip to Egypt with my mother to thank her for all her support. Looking back, I had been in this great country for five years and managed to earn a degree from an Ivy League School, visited Egypt, started a young family, and I was about to start a career in engineering, designing fighter jets for the mighty US Air Force.

I reported to Fairchild the first week of January 1983. The company helped me with lodging and placed me in a hotel for a month. Nidda and Javier were still living full time in upstate New York, and they joined me as soon as I found an apartment in Queens, NY.

My first assignment was in the landing gear division of the A-10A aircraft. The A-10 was already in service. Our job was to continuously improve the design based on field performance. My new boss was Al, and we had a team of about eight to ten engineers. I stayed there for a few months until the company needed an engineer in the armaments/weapons section, where I was then, assigned. I enjoyed that division's work, and we had a tight group of only six engineers, including Roman Woloszyn, who became a friend for life.

The only problem: we had a terrible boss, who I will call Dick, an older fellow.

Just about every top leader has had a bad boss. As unpleasant as this experience is, it's valuable: it teaches you how not to be a leader. You learn the behaviors that will create animosity and poor morale, and years later when you're in a position of influence, you do everything possible to avoid these behaviors.

When Dick came to work, he seemed to find pleasure in giving me and my colleagues a hard time. I thought I could handle Dick, but I was wrong. I tried to be nice to him, but he would have none of that. When I and my colleagues would return one minute late from a break, he would become angry, glancing at his watch, and shaking his head. We knew we could make up the work either by staying a few minutes later or arriving earlier to work the next day, but this was unacceptable to Dick. He just wanted us to be at our desks during designated work hours. He made us mad, and we drove him insane.

One of the projects I really enjoyed was working on the gun gas diverter for the monster 30mm gun of the A-10. When this monster weapon fired, gas would spew out into the engine and stall the airplane. Battelle Labs designed a device that would deflect the gas below the aircraft. I was the engineer who was supposed to integrate the Battelle device into the aircraft. Because of my work on this project, Fairchild wanted to assign me to more classified projects, but I could not get a security clearance because I wasn't a US citizen. Together with my mother and younger sister, Lydia, we completed our applications for US citizenship, got called to the Orange County Court in Goshen, New York, and then, raised our right hand, recited the necessary words, and became American citizens.

Starting to Lead

I kept up with martial arts training. I would go to Spring Valley every weekend to practice with Grand Master Kim. On Saturday, he would have a special class for black belts only. At times, we would do no kicking or any exercise at all. Grand Master would teach us about life and eastern philosophy for the entire session.

This martial arts training had a spillover effect to work, and it helped me be seen as a young leader. Our director of engineering decided he wanted to make the company a friendlier place for young engineers, so he met with us, requesting our ideas that might help achieve this objective. I asked a few questions during the Q&A session, and then presented the director with some options on possible improvements. My colleagues congratulated me on my questions and thought process, and because I was the martial arts instructor for some of them, they treated me with a bit more respect than their other peers. It was not respect that I demanded or even for which I asked. It was a natural result of the relationships I'd established at work and through martial arts.

Though I had never taken a formal course in leadership, Taekwondo provided me with principles for both life and leadership. At Grand Master Kim's Taekwondo school, we had to memorize ten guiding tenets, and I taught them to my class:

1. Be loyal to your country.
2. Be obedient to your parents.
3. Be loving between husband and wife.
4. Be faithful to your friends.
5. Be respectful to your elders.
6. Be cooperative between neighbors.
7. Establish trust between teacher and student.
8. Use good judgment before killing any living things.
9. Never retreat in battle.
10. Always finish what you start.

Fairchild was looking for a representative young engineer to be the conduit between the senior engineers and us. I was unofficially nominated to be their representative. We had permission to use the conference room whenever we needed to meet. For our first meeting for the young engineers, I had posters made and invited all the young engineers to the conference room. Prior to the meeting, I talked to Ken, the director of engineering, and invited him to come down and say a few words. That gesture gave us legitimacy and proved to the young engineers that I had the backing of upper management and was a direct link between them and upper engineering management for issues they did not want to take to their supervisors. The director of engineering added my name to the list of official correspondence between him and the senior managers, giving me access to executive level topics that I could discuss with our group during monthly meetings.

Early on, I discovered the value of showing initiative – of addressing issues that needed to be addressed. As professionals, we did not belong to any union. But as a group distinct from the senior staff, we had no way to pass non-work related concerns to upper management. We started losing young engineers to other engineering firms like Rockwell, Boeing, and Grumman. The director of engineering called me into his office and asked me to discover why our young engineers were leaving the company. I began surveying them about professional challenges and what they saw as other opportunities. I would relate those findings to upper management who were trying to address the issues they were raising. Our group of young engineers also got together after work on some Thursdays at a local pub for socializing. Our bond was getting stronger. I was elected the first president of the Fairchild Young Engineers Association.

Coincidentally, Fairchild was competing to build the next generation jet trainer for the US Air Force, and we worked on the T-46, with side-by-side seating. I was then assigned to the ground test team. My immediate supervisor and co-worker was a man named Dominick Capuano. I enjoyed the quality of the work and the independence Dominick and I had to build our "iron horse." We took all the designs of the flights systems and created an iron frame to place for ground testing – this helped ensure that all worked according to specifications; no parts occupied the same space. With this approach, we also could recommend design changes to our engineers. We were basically doing systems engineering.

Working with experienced experts like Dominick was a great way to learn and to figure out my career path. Dominick had served in World War II and his dad had served in World War I, and he told me stories about these experiences. Many of the stories had to do with the sea, and these tales captured my imagination. Around this time, Nidda was pregnant with our second child, which meant we needed to find a larger living space. It was also the time when the production of the A-10A was just about complete, and the Air Force was hinting that they might choose the design of our competitors instead.

The Next Job

From both personal and professional perspectives, I needed to make a change. As often happens early in careers, I started looking in one direction and fate directed me in another. I began exploring my options as a result of attending an American Institute of Aeronautics and Astronautics (AIAA) aerospace conference, acting as a representative of our company to answer technical questions. The Grumman Aerospace table was right next to us. I met a nice gentleman who was the manager of the testing section at Grumman for both the E-2C Hawkeye and the F-14 Tomcat. I told him I would be interested in touring his test lab, and he gave me his business card.

Shortly thereafter, I visited him, bringing my resume at his request. I also interviewed with other companies, including

Rockwell Aerospace and Bell Helicopter. But for reasons, none of the jobs was right for me (or I wasn't right for them). At Grumman, however, I saw their test lab and fell in love with it. They built naval aircraft, and I wanted to work in a top-notch test lab for the Navy. I had heard a lot of good things about the Navy from a friend, and my colleague, Dominick, was a Navy guy.

I recognized that I needed to switch jobs to remain marketable. I had been at Fairchild for almost three years, and a number of other young engineers had already left. Grumman made me a good offer, but before I accepted it, Dominick told me I should join the Navy or the Air Force. Though I insisted I wasn't a military type – I wasn't one to follow orders blindly – I had great respect for Dominick and decided to follow his advice.

I made an appointment to talk to an Air Force recruiter. I told the recruiter that I would like to design airplanes for the US Air Force. I asked him about the requirements, and he told me that I would have to take the tests, sign up, go to Air Force training, and that depending on how I did after the training boot camp would determine my Air Force assignment. The more I thought about it, the more downside I saw – I could receive a job and position that I might hate. So, I decided to investigate the Navy.

Chapter 3

The Arduous Journey
from Air to Sea

I drove to Hempstead, for an interview with a young Navy lieutenant by the name of Ray Baltera; I still have a picture of him. He gave me a general test, which took an approximately an hour. I passed. I then took and passed the aviation test with outstanding results. I told the lieutenant that not only could I answer the test questions but could design the parts to make them better. He was impressed. He proceeded to show me some short clips about aircraft carriers and jets taking off. I was impressed.

Lieutenant Baltera asked if I would like to visit the cradle of naval aviation, all expenses paid. If I liked it, then I should come back, and we'd have another discussion.

I flew to Pensacola, Florida, and was picked up by a team of two recruiters. There were six potential recruits for the weekend. The next day after a tour of the base, we went to the Naval Aviation Museum where we were told about naval aviation. Later, we watched the Blue Angels practicing. That evening, we went to the famous Pensacola Officer Club. It was vibrant and full of life. I was sold!

When I returned to New York, I met with Lieutenant Baltera again and asked to take the oath, which I did on April 4, 1985. Lieutenant Baltera told me I could do design work for the Navy as an aerospace duty engineer, but I would have to get my wings first by flying for the Navy. In the Navy, engineers are aviators first, so they know and understand the intricacies of the systems for which they were responsible. That was a deal I could live with – I could do that.

I drove to Pensacola, and on the way, I thought about the toughness of the program I was about to enter. I had seen the movie *An Officer and a Gentleman*, and I knew the challenges ahead. One of the great secrets of leadership is contained in the Boy Scouts motto: Always be prepared. I was prepared mentally and physically. Once I signed up, I started to jog and run in the mornings and after work. As I drove to Pensacola, I would pull over on the shoulder of Route 13, lock the car, run a mile or so, and run back, just so I could keep in shape.

Driving through the South, I saw more Black people than I saw in New York or New Jersey. I had heard about lynchings and all the other stuff White folks did to Black people in the South. I told my mother that those things were in the past, though she was convinced that they were still happening. Because I had no experience with that aspect of American life, I decided to be careful.

I arrived in the town of Pensacola and made my way to the base. I arrived and checked in at the designated location. They placed me in G-Company. The G-Company leader, another candidate waiting to start class, took us to chow, gave us a tour of the immediate area, and told us what to expect. I had arrived early and had about one month before the official instruction began. My priority during this time was to become a better swimmer – a key skill for a naval officer. Though I grew up near the ocean, I never had any formal swimming lessons. I would be in the pool for five to six hours a day. During this month, I also found a nearby apartment for my family.

The other activity I and the other candidates pursued was scoping out drill instructors. We learned which one was tough, which one was good, and which one to stay away from. I thought the best one of them all was Gunnery Sergeant Crenshaw, USMC. He was tall, hard as nails, and feared, but he was fair. I saw him at work. He gave his class his all, but the class had to have the guts to take it. If they couldn't take it, he kicked them out. That is why I wanted him.

The best leaders want to be challenged, and to be challenged by the best. I knew if I was able to hang in there, he would shape me into a lean, mean, fighting machine.

You didn't know who your drill instructor would be until the very morning of the class. Finally, I was told that my class would start on Monday. I was to detach G-Company on Sunday after-noon, join the incoming students, and wait for further instructions. I had seen about four or five classes go through the routine, and now it was finally my turn. I was ready.

A Harsh Initiation

That Sunday, I did not report to G-Company. I reported with the class that was to start the next day. The first step in our transfor-mation was to strip us of anything and everything that would remind us of our old identity as civilians. From that point on, our drill instructors owned us until further notice. Our "poopie suits" consisted of a chrome dome; gray, shiny, ugly looking cover; a white t-shirt; and greenish Cammy pants. From that moment on, every minute of our life was scheduled and calculated.

We were each assigned to a room, four candidates per room. The class had about ninety people. Bedtime was at 2200. We were sent to our room by 2130 and told to be ready for tomorrow. Tomorrow, we would meet the one person who for the next ninety days would be our father, our mother, our counselor, our teacher, our everything. We were told to be on the station within seconds once we were awoken. I slept in my shirt, underwear, and socks. I placed my sneakers on the floor right in front of my bed. I strategically placed my Cammy pants right on top of the sneakers so I could jump into them when the time came and land right into my sneakers. I rehearsed that movement a few times and got it down pat. By then, it was 2200, and I laid on my rack, anticipating the next morning. I did not know what to expect, but I was ready to face it head on. And then I drifted to sleep with thoughts of how far I had come from Haiti flowing through my brain.

I awoke to human thunder, bellows of "Everyone get the hell up!" I jumped off my bed into my pants, slid into my sneakers, ran out the door, made a quick left, and was in line in the hallway next to the person who got there just prior to me. As we waited, people were still making their way to the hallway. We had been instructed to look straight ahead, standing at attention, with zero movement. We were aware of the presence of the drill instructor in his sharp and impeccable Marine uniform and his Smokey hat.

He was fuming and calm, and he had energy. As we all lined up, he said, "Side, straddle up!" and we began doing jumping jacks. We probably did fifty or one hundred, I do not know because I lost count. Then he ordered, "Down, give me fifty," and we did fifty push-ups. "Upside, straddle up," and we did a few hundred. "Down, gimme fifty," and we did another hundred. "Now you are warmed up, on your back! Leg lift, six inches off the deck," and we held it six inches from the deck for ten seconds, fifty seconds, one minute, two minutes...who knows how long it was. Then the command "Ninety!" and we took our legs ninety degrees up. "Up on your feet." We got up and stood at attention. The deck was nothing but a pool of sweat. The drill instructor introduced himself:

"From now on, I will be your mother, I will be your father, I will be your ... hey you, why are you staring at me? Everybody on the deck, gimme fifty, another fifty, and another, and another! Back up, on your feet. When I talk to you, you will look straight ahead and will not stare at me, do you understand?"

"Yes sir," we screamed on the top of our lungs? "I cannot hear you!" "Yes sir." "Hell, can't you guys speak loud enough for me to hear you?" We started to get the drift, no matter how loud you scream, no matter what you do, you will screw up, and you will pay.

With hindsight and for anyone who wasn't in the military, this may seem like an overly harsh approach to training, even a bit sadistic. But from a leadership perspective, this "tear-you-down-to-build-you-up" experience is necessary. Even most non-military people experience the equivalent of a tough drill instructor early in their careers. They work for a boss who comes down hard on them for mistakes, who criticizes harshly and sometimes personally. At the time, it's a miserable experience. Later in a career, though, most people recognize the value of this experience. They realize the importance of being humbled, of realizing how much there is to learn and being motivated to learn it. It gives them insight about the mindsets of people just starting out, and it provides them with a degree of humility that is necessary for strong leadership.

Back then, of course, I lacked this wisdom and instead was focused on doing whatever was necessary to make it through training. I decided not to mentally question anything the drill instructor said or ordered. I was on autopilot for immediate execution. Later, I would realize the military value of this drill instructor's methods: to by-pass people's reflexive questioning of an order. The drill instructor wanted us to respond to his orders with instantaneous execution – any delay might endanger our lives or those of others when we were officers. From the time he said, "gimme …," he expected everybody on the deck already on their second or third push up, before he even finished with the word "… fee-tee." I was there; I was fully engaged. And finally, he'd shout, "You slimy worms will go, take a shower, shave, and get dressed. I will be outside waiting for you. You have five minutes. The last person to report will have hell to pay. Do not be the last person … you will have hell to pay! Ready–Dismiss!"

We all ran to the showers. There was instantaneous coordination, as some guys jumped under the showers two or three at a
time. The first one would get wet, and step out to soap up, as
another one would jump under the same shower head to get wet
and so on. When I finished, I ran to my room and changed, took
my chrome dome and ran out the door. Ran the steps and out I
was, in front of the building. I was not the last one out, but there
were quite a few already in line. How did they do it? No matter
how fast I was, someone was always faster.

I felt sorry for the last guy who came out. Gunny always did
what he said he would do. I believe that was part of the trust
building process. It was drilled into us that Gunny had an impeccable memory; that Gunny knew everything. He said he would
tell us when to breathe, when to think, when to shower, when
to eat, when to wake up, when to do anything. He said that we
belonged to him!

We lined up in front of the chow hall along the wall with the
first person barely in front of the door. When ordered to enter, the
first candidate would step forward with the left foot, instantly pivoting ninety degrees on that same left foot, step forward with the
right foot, as the right foot hits the plank forming the frame of the
doorway, he would sound off, "Zero one!" the next candidates
would sound off like clockwork. We seemed to get it, until we got
to ten and that candidate paused for an extra second before
sounding off.

Gunny shouted, "Hell, no! What did I just hear? A whole
bunch of slimy college grads who can't even count! Everybody, get
out, get the hell out of my chow hall, and start over again. Line up!
You will obey my orders and execute exactly the way you are told.
It will be like clockwork, without skipping a beat. Otherwise, you
will all get back to the street and will give me one thousand push-
ups." Because Gunny said one thousand, he meant one thousand.

We had ninety people to get through that door and there was
no way we were going to get it right the first time, no matter how
much and how well we concentrated. I thought I was a hot shot

engineer from Cornell. Then I realized that I was nothing when I made a mistake sounding off – I could not even count. The drill instructor finally allowed us to get in line for food, though we were not allowed to talk in line. We sat with our food and were told, "You can pray to whatever or whomever you want, but you will wait the order to pray when ready." There was not one sound in the room. Everyone was sitting at attention. The drill instructor paced slowly and said, "I will give the order of execution and say 'Ready, pray.' Upon hearing that order, you will answer 'Snap,' and immediately bow your head forward and you will pray. Then I will say, 'Ready eat,' and everyone will start eating at the same time. You will finish everything in your plate. I will personally inspect your plate and will ensure you swallow everything on your plate. Failure to do so will cost you, and you will have hell to pay." Of course, we didn't get it right and there was a hell to pay.

By the time the first week was over, we were down to fifty people. At least twenty said the magic word, D-O-R. That is all it takes to get a break, for the punishment to stop. It only took three words, and all the preparations, all the punishments, and a bright future ahead would just vanish. DOR meant "dropped on request."

The Water Test

Like many aspiring leaders, I was eager to test my limits. I wanted to see how far I could go, and how much punishment I could endure. Our day consisted of academics, physical training, swimming, and other activities. At about the fourth week, the time came for the final swimming test. We had to demonstrate the various strokes, side stroke, breaststroke, back stroke, American crawl, and so on. Then we had to swim a mile or so in flight gear. Jump from a 50-feet tower and swim underwater for a certain distance. The final exercise was to swim in place in full gear, fully loaded with combat boots, helmets, parachutes, and tread water for five minutes.

It was exhausting, especially after a full day of events. Then we had to transition to "drown-proof," where one plays dead and comes up for a single breath after every few seconds or so. I transitioned to it with no problem. Suddenly, my heart started pounding. I tried to control it by taking a nice slow breath and going back down under water, but my heart kept beating faster. I wanted to take full breath and keep on breathing.

The instructors noticed that something was going on with me. They encouraged me to slow down and stick with it. I submerged for another breath and then, I felt that I was going to explode. My brain told me to get out of the water; another little voice told me to hang on, I could do it. My instinct to preserve my life battled with my cognition, which told me that I had to stay in the water if I wanted to pass. It was a fight-or-flight decision. I knew in my mind that I could do it, because I had done it several times before in practice; except this time, it was the real test. I told myself that there are several safety swimmers in the water and that they will not let me die. My instinctive voice, though, was much stronger. My heart kept beating faster, and faster; I felt that it was going to burst through my chest.

Throughout a career, leaders will face at least one crucial decision. They will be under extreme pressure and time constraints, and a lot will be riding on their decision. Experiences such as this one prepared me for ones down the road. I was facing what felt like a life-or-death situation with only a few seconds to decide. There was no one to lean on, no one to offer advice.

In this instance, I decided that I was getting out of the water. Once doubt settles in, it is extremely hard to recover. I panicked and swam toward safety. I had been drown-proofing for four minutes, one more minute and I would have passed. By the time I pulled myself up and took those crucial breaths I longed for, the lead instructor called "Time" and everyone else got out of the water. They explained the situation to me. I would repeat the same, treading water/drown-proofing exercise tomorrow. If I could not complete the test then, I would pack my bag and go home.

I went through the rest of the day with the other students. I tried not to think about what just happened. Soon enough it was

2200 and time for bed. I kept thinking to myself that all I had to do was to relax; just do what I was taught. I kept convincing myself that the safety instructors were there and watching my every move. They would not let me die and would pull me out of the water if I passed out and before I drowned.

Trusting my life completely to someone else was a huge mental step. We are born with the instinct to preserve our life; it is in our DNA. To do the contrary is completely against human nature and requires rigorous training. That night I spoke to God: Please give me the strength tomorrow to prevail, help me control my breathing, and do not let me get out of the water until I pass the test. As I continued to pray, I fell asleep.

I awoke the next morning, with an unnatural calmness. I went for breakfast in formation, executed the plan of the day, and at the time took my swim gear and reported to the swimming pool. I put on my flight suit, heavy aviator boots, parachute, and then all the other extra survival gear. I was not the only one to have gotten out of the water – a few others were also re-taking the test.

Once again, I plunged into the water with the impossibly heavy equipment. This time, though, I focused on controlling my breathing. My life had taught me resilience and resolve; that it was always possible to succeed after failure if you approached the challenge the right way. I treaded water calmly, concentrating on each stroke. I found myself silently reciting Psalm 23 in French, timing the verse to the movement of my hands, establishing a cadence: "L'éternel est mon berger" (the Lord is my shepherd); two strokes, "Je ne manquerai de rien" (I will fear no evil). Then I heard the instructor's voice: "Drown-proof!" Down I went, sinking like an iron anchor, but I continued my silent recitation. Up and down, I went, treading water and then sinking when the command was given, the bible verses keeping me calm and focused. It was as if I were meditating and had reached a state of transcendence. Even after I had passed the test, I requested permission to continue treading water, and then simulating drowning. The surprised instructor granted my request. By transcending my fear, I was in what positive psychology pioneer Mihaly Csikszentmihalyi refers to as flow. I had mastered a scary, difficult assignment with my mind, not just my body.

Leaders do more than they think they can. We possess the capacity for over achievement. Just as I found the strength inside of me to pass the test, we all possess something — a bible verse, a poem, the wisdom of a mentor, a parent's repeated advice — that we can draw upon in challenging moments.

Life-changing Events

It was a day like any other day in training. We were in the middle of conducting rifle drills. As usual, we could not get it right and were being punished together as a class. We were holding the M16 rifle by the butt in our extended right hand. It was hard to keep the arm straight with that much weight on one hand, but we were trying. Then one of the candidate officers approached the drill instructor and told him something. The instructor asked me to accompany the candidate officer, who said he was taking me to the Pensacola hospital where my wife was about to deliver my second child. Exhausted and exhilarated, I got in the car without changing and went to the hospital. On my way there, my wife had already delivered my son. I went in and gave her a big kiss. I picked up my son, as Nidda asked me what we shall call him. I thought about it a little bit, for we had not discussed a possible name yet, and then suggested we call him Maurice, in honor of my father with the middle name, Valentino, in honor of Professor Valentin, my violin teacher. It was then time to get back to training. Though excited about the birth of my son, I could not lose focus.

I made it through the rest of the rigorous training. It was a complete transformation from being civilian personnel to becoming a military officer in the most powerful military organization that ever existed.

Graduation day was memorable; we marched in formation and then went to the chapel where we were pinned as ensigns in the

US Navy and rewarded with the Gold Bar! As I exited the chapel door, Gunnery Sergeant Crenshaw, United States Marine Corps, was the very first person waiting for us outside under the flagpole. There, we all received our very first salute as officers. I still believed that I still needed to salute Gunny Crenshaw, and I knew I would believe it until I died.

Just about every leader has an early mentor or at least a professional role model. Even though this individual may put people through hell, they imparts lessons worth learning. The characteristics he worked so hard to instill in us, the energy he infused in us, have lasted me a lifetime. Later, I realized how lucky I was. Just because someone is your boss doesn't mean that they're a good boss with qualities worth emulating.

Some drill instructors weren't good or were mediocre at best. Gunny Crenshaw, however, poured his heart and soul into those he was given in charge. He went above and beyond to ensure that critical leadership principles were infused in us not just through words but through his example – every gesture, every run, every four-letter word spiced up with his spit as he stood one inch from my face screaming and exposing my faults and weaknesses in front of my colleagues helped me learn and grow. He communicated that I still had a long way to go as a leader. He showed me that life was a journey, and that leadership development was a lifelong enterprise. He developed in me an insatiable desire for excellence. Nothing that I do would ever be good enough. No matter how hard I tried, he showed me that I could always go one step further. When I thought I was giving my very best and I had no more to give, he showed me that I had a lot in reserve.

To Fly or Fix

I took a few days off and then reported to VT-10 for continued aviation training. I went through ground school and then flight training. I did not really know what airplanes to select. Many of my peers opted for jets, but the plane type mattered less to me than where I would be training. I selected to go to P-3 because it gave me the chance to take my family west to California and Mather Air Force Base.

The training went well. My initial reason for joining the Navy was to fix things, and I still wanted to work on engines, design planes, and do engineering. The higher-ups told me to be an aviation engineering duty officer, I would have to fly for five years after getting my gold wings. And then, I could apply for the Aerospace Engineering Duty Officer (AEDO) program, but there was no guarantee that I would be accepted. This uncertainty caused me to explore other options within the Navy. I found out about the Surface Warfare Officer (SWO) program, where officers get to do engineering, work on their gear, or at least directly supervise their maintenance. I talked to a few people who told me the way to get into that program was to drop out of aviation and fill out an application for SWO. I went to my skipper and discussed the possibility with him. He thought I was crazy – why in the world would I do that? He said there are at least 200 highly qualified applicants waiting for my spot as a naval aviator.

With only two or three more months to go in the program, I would soon be home free as an aviator for life. What the skipper may not have known is that many great leaders don't take the easy path. Instead, they search for the right path, no matter how difficult, challenging, or dangerous it might be.

It wasn't just that I wanted to fix planes; I didn't enjoy flying as much as many of my peers. Maybe that was because I didn't grow up with dreams of being a pilot, having taken my first flight at the late age of nineteen. The skipper told me to hang in there, and I would learn to enjoy it. I had just finished Daytime Celestial (Day-Cel) navigation, and then I had a month of Night Celestial navigation, one final month for maritime or over water navigation, and then I would graduate.

I had been in the program for over a year and now had a crucial decision to make. If I got my wings, I would have to fly for five years. I told the skipper I was dropping out. He actually thought something was wrong (mentally) with me and had me see a doctor, who found that I was normal (and in his report, noted that I "was looking for a more challenging line of work").The skipper called for a board to formally hear my case.

Despite these and other distractions, I maintained my focus – a skill that helped me then, and helped me as a leader for years to come.When the board heard my case, board members tried to dissuade me, explaining that there were countless numbers of people who would kill to be a naval aviator. But I was adamant about my decision.They thought I was making the mistake of a lifetime, but I believed that I was searching for my destiny.

Making a Controversial Switch

I was temporarily assigned to the computer group in charge of designing and updating the flight routes for the students, which I enjoyed. I filled out my application to become a ship driver and waited patiently. I was accepted and had to report to Newport, Rhode Island, by January 1986. I left California and drove to Newport. I flew my wife and children to New Jersey to be with her parents, while I focused on learning all about ships.

It was my first time in Newport, and this would not be the last time. It was a big class and I was assigned to Section 12, with the students whose last names started with S, T, and Us. It was like drinking from a fire hydrant. Surface Warfare Officer School, or SWOSDOC as they called it, was six months of intense shipboard training. SWOSDOC was an intensive course with so much to learn and so little time. I would go back to the classroom every night after class to study. We took our first test, and I passed with flying colors. Those who did not do well were put on "mando" (mandatory study), and I voluntarily joined them. When ship selection time came, I requested assignment to a cruiser in the engineering department.

Little did I know that most people tried to stay away from the engineering department, because it had a fleet reputation of backbreaking work. But I've never been afraid of hard work and in fact, relish it. I was assigned to USS Biddle (CG 34), a 1,200-pound steam cruiser (pressure system). I was told the ship was in the Philadelphia Naval Shipyard. I sent the required letter of introduction to the captain and told him how much I was looking forward to reporting aboard – I did not get a reply but was not expecting one.

After graduation, I reported to the engineering school and pursued another intensive course of instruction. There, I learned about boilers, machinery, valves, and pipes. It was heaven. Suddenly, everything I learned at Cornell started making sense to me. I was being introduced to the practical application of pure engineering and science. We learned the engineering principles behind such a piece of gear, and then we would see the gear in operation. I could visualize a drop of water and how it was scooped from the ocean by the main condenser, through a main valve, creating a vacuum after passing through a heat exchanger and back into the ocean again. I could also envision the path through the boiler's economizer, until water became steam through the steam tubes and went all the way to the engines as this super-heated air made the turbines spin. It was fascinating stuff, and I loved every minute of it. One of my school instructors was a certain LT Bill Crow, a tall and very interesting professor who taught the topic on a basic engineering system as "sump-pump-dump-strainer-cooler-bearing."

In September 1987, I graduated from Engineering Officer of the Watch (EOOW) School and immediately reported to USS Biddle (CG 34) in Norfolk, Virginia. My first mission upon reporting was to find a place for my family to live – a three-bedroom house, not too far from the beach. We moved in, and my wife quickly turned it into our home for the next three years.

Chapter 4

Underway: The First Journey as a Ship and as an Officer

In September 1987, I reported to my very first ship in the US Navy, the USS Biddle. The ship had been in overhaul in the Philadelphia Naval Shipyard for over a year, getting a new weapon system named New Threat Upgrade (NTU), which was design-based on the Russian tactics against US aircraft carriers. I eventually discovered that most of the focus was on the combat system and not a lot of attention was dedicated to the engineering plant.

When I reported, I assumed that someone would be there to welcome me on board; I was mistaken. I looked for the officer that I would relieve and found him. He was a Naval Academy graduate and a very busy officer. He said they did not have a stateroom for me yet and would assign me to the Junior Officer (JO) Jungle for now. He took me to the unmade rack of a chief warrant officer (CWO) who left the ship a few days ago, and there I settled myself. I made the bed per the Navy regulations that I had just learned at SWOS but realized no other rack or bed was made per regulation.

I learned my first organizational lesson; one that applies to businesses as well as the military: A delta exists between what they are teaching in the schoolhouse and what is happening in the fleet.

Learning on the Job

I checked in with my new boss, the chief engineer, and at first I liked him. Like me, he had gone through naval aviator training, so we had something in common. He seemed to know his engineering; therefore, I was looking forward to learning a lot from him.

We were scheduled to get underway for a week off the Virginia Capes to conduct weapon system testing. I was assigned a watch as Engineering Officer of the Watch (EOOW), receiving instruction from Larry. He had a port and starboard watch, which means he was on watch from midnight to 0600 and off from 0600 to noon. He came on again at noon until 1800 and was off until he took over again at midnight. I thoroughly enjoyed my first watch underway, watching the EOOW bring the plant to life and following the strict and intense coordination of all the other watch sections. For me, it was engineering heaven – I could not have been happier. Because of my previous engineering schooling, I understood what was going on in the plant. I could mentally follow the steps and could visualize a drop of water making its way from the feedwater tank, to the economizer, down through the tubes, turning into vapor and steam, and making its way into the engine room to impinge on the main engine propeller. From there, its longitudinal energy turned the blades as it transformed into rotational energy – that was fascinating stuff. That was everything I learned coming alive right in front of me.

I learned the rhythms and responsibilities of my position relative to others on the ship. The executive officer (XO) would meet with the department heads in the wardroom for about ten minutes, while division officers and chiefs formed up by departments in some part of the ship. Each department had their own spot for departmental and divisional quarters. Meanwhile, the divisions would also assemble and get instructions and specific work assignments from the senior first-class petty officers.

My previous lesson was being reinforced: There was a lot of how it is supposed to be done versus how it really is done. One had to learn the ropes – the way things really worked – and only then, could you become a salty dog.

Given all the watches and responsibilities, I averaged three hours of sleep daily or nightly. I found out that the working hours for a shipboard engineer are bestial. With hindsight, I realized why most people at SWOS thought I was crazy for volunteering to go to a ship's engineering department, especially a 1,200-pounder. Yet, I enjoyed it and tackled my assignments enthusiastically. I walked around the ship and met many of my colleagues, but I still had not met the XO and the commanding officer (CO), the two people on top of the food chain onboard any warship. I was eager to obtain their guidance, and I made an appointment to see the XO, arriving thirty minutes early.

Unfortunately, others also needed to see him too, and eventually I was told to come back later. Having been on board for a month without seeing the XO, I felt I had failed in the sense that I had not finished my check-in process. For this reason, I cornered the XO in a passageway with my check-in sheet. I told him I had not been able to secure an appointment with him and asked him to sign my check-in sheet. He stopped, barely looking at me or saying any-thing, signed it, and moved on. This may sound as if he was being rude, but the XO is the busiest person onboard a ship.

My next task would be to see the old man – the captain. Because the XO was responsible for scheduling the CO's time, I approached him again and made my request; he told me he would get back to me.

I was hanging around the division, but I was not really the division officer yet. I was going to be assigned as boilers officer and the two firerooms had a lot of engineering problems resulting from neglect during the shipyard period. When I went down there, I felt more like I was in the way. I had no guidance nor direction on what

I was supposed to do, and it appeared that the chief had everything under control. This was frustrating, but I tried to conduct my own inspections to do something useful.

A new XO arrived, and he was a tough man. He was a nuclear trained officer – we called him "a nuke" – but I found out that he did not like that moniker; he preferred "nuclear-trained officers." My first encounter with the new XO was when I brought him my list of issues I'd discovered on my own. He went through the roof, insisting he would not sign it; he explained that we could all get fired for such a list. I did not understand! I did not make up the list. It was the result of crawling under equipment, looking at uncalibrated gauges and various other issues that existed throughout the plant.

It was another early lesson: People want problems fixed rather than "broadcast" on a page where everyone can see what is wrong and have to answer for it. I realized that there was a lot of learning by deduction onboard a ship.

I also learned how to deal with "difficult" officers – a skill all future leaders need as their careers progress. My senior chief wasn't happy with me being his division officer. Every time I talked to him, he would raise his hand like a traffic cop, instructing me to stop. If I asked him a question about the division, he responded like I was bothering him. I had studied what my responsibilities were as the division officer. The manual listed at least 300 different responsibilities. I was ready to accomplish each and every one, but no one was willing or able to give me clear guidance on expectations. I realized that I was on my own.

The department head did not help either. When equipment broke, he would call and order me to write a casualty report message (CASREP) to order the broken part. But how did he know a part was broken? Who told him? How did he know before me? As a division officer, my job was to find out the status of broken equipment in my division and report it to my department head. Again, I approached senior chief, and again he raised his hand in negation of my request. A division should follow his chain of command by going to his division officer first, but what if the chief is not cooperating?

I tried to find a work-around so I could do my job properly. I would go to where the broken equipment was and speak to the guys hard at work trying to fix it, but they were too busy fixing the gear and did not have time to explain to me what was wrong. I felt useless. I would manage to get scraps of information and be able to order the parts to fix the equipment.

In a cruiser, the XO is the president of the mess, and the CO eats in his cabin alone. He had his own wardroom mess and his own cook. Though the CO was occasionally invited to have lunch with us, I would be either on watch or in the plant and had missed the first few meals with the captain. Finally, I was in the wardroom when he arrived for lunch, and as he came around to say hello to his officers, he looked at me and said, "And, who are you?" I told him that I was his boilers officer. He did not ask any further questions.

The captain was not a big talker. He would drive his Cadillac all the way up to the pier, park it in front of the ship, and go up to his cabin. He would stay there until the end of the workday, about 1500 or so, and we would hear the four bells and the gong, which meant that the CO had departed for the day. His presence onboard did not affect me; my only contact with him was when I would present him with CASREPs for his signature, and he would sign without asking any questions or saying much to me at all. Our captain was then the most senior captain in the East coast, and the new combat system was his baby.

Leaders may have achieved a lot, but they may still be seriously flawed.

Training at GTMO

When we were preparing to journey to Guantanamo Bay, Cuba (GTMO), for training, we lit the boilers and a tube ruptured. Everything went to hell in a handbasket. The amount of work doubled, and the boiler technicians were working late every day to get it fixed. We were working long, arduous hours.

Once we repaired the ruptured tube, we got underway, and it was a relief. Moving on our ship to our destination, we could derive comfort from our routines – standing watches, eating the good Navy chow, and sleeping.

Once we reached GTMO, we began training. There was a saying that in GTMO, "yoke is no joke." Each division has someone assigned to go and check every single door, hatch, opening, and access to and from the ship. After visual verification, the assigned individual goes to Damage Control Central and signs for the division. In GTMO, they would call for the setting of Yoke, and after it was set, people would pass the word that "Yoke is set throughout the ship," and the inspectors would verify the proper setting. Typically, they would find hundreds of valves and accesses in improper positions, whether closed or open. We would try again, and again we would fail.

There were several reasons to explain this failure. A ship has thousands of accesses and openings. Each division is assigned a few hundred. Given all the variables, things can easily go wrong. Yoke was just one of hundreds of training exercises at GTMO. We also tested the combat systems and shot a few missiles in the range. Upon returning home, we were a crew well-trained in the basics and were now qualified to start the training cycle that would finish with the Joint Fleet Training Exercise. Training was the key to survival, and we trained as if for a fight, because we knew that we would fight exactly as we trained.

Details matter. Some people suggest you shouldn't sweat the small stuff. You don't want to get wrapped up in the most minor matters and neglect the major ones. At the same time, good leaders recognize that small things add up to be big things. Paying attention to details is important, whether you're running a ship or a business.

During one of our fleet training exercises, we had the pleasure of testing our NTU weapon system against the best – the new and state-of-the-art Aegis Weapon system. We went to the missile range with two Aegis cruisers in the middle of our naval formation. We got the call that the threat missile was away, and we picked it up in our radar and shot while the cruisers were still waiting to engage. The flag officer onboard our ship had us delay our next shot by a few seconds even though we had a clear shot at the incoming target; he wanted to give the other two ships an opportunity to fire. NTU beat Aegis. NTU's downfall was the ship's engineering plant; we had an old platform and Aegis was a brand-new cruiser. Aegis also possessed a superior computer power system. We had one main computer with redundant components to control the entire combat system, and Aegis had seven of these same computers.

Sometimes, the tried-and-true can be more effective than the brand-spanking new.

Getting Down and Dirty

In the coming months, I spent a lot of time in the engineering plant. Our objective was to fully grasp the makeup, design, and working of each major engineering piece of equipment onboard the ship, and then achieve the same working level of knowledge for each major system.

There was an enormous amount to learn and pressure to learn it quickly. I remember being observed by Senior Chief Chris Romeii as I was standing watch in the Number 1 Engine Room. I had to trace the system, go to the main condenser to identify every opening, valves, access doors, and even every possible vent. Then I returned to the senior chief and recited from memory the working of this intricate piece of gear. I did it successfully, but at that rate I began to wonder how long it would take to master all the knowledge necessary to pass the EOOW board. I estimated that I would need at least three years, which would be the end of my tour on the ship. And there were still other areas of knowledge I needed to learn; I couldn't imagine how I would be qualified in every system on board the ship to become an SWO.

After about six or seven months, I felt I was ready for the EOOW board in front of the captain.

On the day of the board, I was very calm and confident. The board was composed of the commanding officer of the ship, the chief engineer, the main propulsion assistant (MPA), and Senior Chief Romeii. They entered the CO's cabin and had a quick conversation while I waited outside the door. I was called in and told to sit down. They proceeded to ask me a series of questions, and I responded with the correct answers. With all my studying and excruciating preparations, I could not only explain the system but tell them what it smelled like – I had crawled around it and all my senses had been engaged.

Finally, the chief engineer, perhaps wanting to impress the captain, started to ask questions about the Main Space Fire Doctrine, which is the main book that the damage control assistant (DCA) uses to fight a major fire onboard the ship. This was outside my area of knowledge and responsibility. How could I know all these things he was talking about? A board usually takes an hour to complete, even the biggest board for final SWO qualification. Mine was going for an hour and a half, and I was still being grilled.

They excused me, and I went outside while the board had its debate and discussion. Eventually, I was summoned back, and the captain said I did not pass. The chief engineer offered his comments – he said I had a lot of book knowledge and lacked deck plate experience. He proposed that I go back down to the plant to get additional deck plate experience. I was flabbergasted. My new chief, as well as the electrician chief, had passed without the width and depth of knowledge that I possessed. Still, I decided that I would do exactly as the chief engineer prescribed.

When my fireroom supervisor, BT1 Reed, learned of the board's decision, he was upset. He said, "Sir, I have been here for almost five years and have seen all the EOOWs being qualified and this is the very first time I have seen them sending anyone for more deck plate experience. I cannot believe that they are sending you to do this. They are doing it to you because you are Black."

First-Class Petty Officer Reed was a White sailor. I'd never considered that racial bias was the problem. Instead, I wondered if my French/Creole accent might have been the issue; and I considered it possible that my superiors did not have full confidence in my abilities. Back then, there was a common perception that if someone had an accent, they weren't as smart as people with typical American speech patterns. But I never thought that it was because I was Haitian and Black.

As I noted earlier, being Haitian was a different experience than being "Black" in the US. We beat the heck out of the French under Napoleon Bonaparte in 1803 and kicked them out of our country just like Americans kicked the British out of America in 1781. We were the second free Republic in the Western Hemisphere. We were as proud of our land as Americans are proud of theirs. The main difference between us was economic.

Ultimately, though, it didn't matter if the chief engineer was biased. I couldn't force him to have confidence in my ability. But I was convinced that I could earn that confidence.

I had to erase all doubt in his mind. I would not accept discrimination as the barrier to my advancement. Discrimination is very subtle and difficult to prove positively or negatively, because the one discriminating may not even be aware of their bias. I would not let myself be mentally bound by negative thoughts and ideas, although I know they existed. I needed to give them irrefutable proof that I could handle the plant just like a White person could.

I asked one of my sharpest firemen, a White young man named Messer, if he would instruct me; he said he'd be delighted to do so. Messer took me every hour with him around the entire fireroom, executing his messenger duty. As division officer, I have seen firemen like Messer do their tours and their rounds. I watched as he read and reread the same gauges, writing down certain critical temperatures. Then he took them to the top watch who had to review everything circled in red. I would ask the top watch, especially BT2 Bruce Jones, one of my favorites, what he was looking for and he would take time to explain the intricacies of operating a boiler while the ship was under way. It was a fascinating world and one to which I had not been privy. I was now seeing the division through their eyes. I was seeing the importance of maintenance and repair, and how they affected operations underway. I spent a week or so under Messer and moved to the next watch. Each station got a bit more complex. I went ahead and lit fire in the boiler and qualified as a burnerman, then as upperlevel and lowerlevel. I stood watch with the top watch. I shadowed several watchstanders – electricians, throttlemen, and others. The guys were starting to feel sorry for me. They kept saying that no chiefs or officers had ever done what I was doing.

After about a year or so aboard in September 1988, I went back to the chief engineer and told him I was ready for my board. He scheduled it with the captain. I walked in ready to deal with any curve ball that the gathered officers might throw. There was no space aboard the engineering plant that I had not walked through or crawled. I knew just about every valve and every piece of piping. The chief engineer said "Captain, I have seen him crawling the spaces and believe he is ready." They did not ask me any engineering question and congratulated me for passing my EOOW board.

Though I was glad I passed, I was also disappointed. They did not even give me the chance to tell them about how many seconds it takes the upperlevelman in the aft fireroom to perform his immediate actions, and the lowerlevelman in the forward fireroom to perform his own emergency procedures during a loss of vacuum in the forward engine room. Unable to awe them with my knowledge, I simply accepted their handshakes.

The obvious lesson here was that leaders are impressed by actions. I had gone above and beyond with my crawling around the ship, and the chief engineer's testimony was all the captain needed to receive a pass. But I also learned something that would prove valuable in the years ahead when I was a leader: There's no substitute for seeing things through other people's eyes. It was one thing to observe from a distance. It was something else entirely to accompany all the men on the line through the ship and work with them as they performed their tasks. Leaders who can see situations through their people's eyes possess much more insight about how everything really works.

Standing Up for My People

It was with the greatest pleasure that I woke up the next morning to go on watch and signed in the log, now able to take the watch by myself. It was a particularly fitting place, as we were off the coast of some island in the Caribbean Sea where the British Fleet and the French Fleet used to roam freely to attack Haiti during their Revolutionary war back in 1791.

I loved my boiler technicians (BTs), all forty of them – even early on, I believed in the importance of forming relationships with my people.

One day we had a shipwide zone inspection, and the XO picked out spaces to inspect. We spent hours cleaning up and waiting for the XO on the upper level of the fireroom. He came down to inspect our bilge without warning, coming down through an escape trunk. The division had worked hard to get ready for the XO. A word or two of encouragement from the XO would have gone a long way toward making the men feel as if their effort had been worth it. Instead, he chastised them for small imperfections.

I gathered the division on the flight deck late in the afternoon. They expected me to scream at them or even withhold their liberty and give them extra wire-brushing duties. Instead, I thanked them for their effort. I told them we did not satisfy leadership this time, but I had confidence that they could do it next time, and I gave them liberty. I decided to send them home, but I would stay behind. If there were any repercussions, I'd deal with it. I felt I had to stand up for my division.

This was the day when I started gaining the trust of the division. They started seeing me not just like another division officer who barked orders, but someone with compassion, respect, and love for them.

I was learning that leaders stick their necks out for their folks. It demonstrates courage, and people respect that quality more than anything.

The Hammer and the Nail

At the same time, I continued to work hard to gain the trust and confidence of my superior officers. One day, the ship pulled into St. Johns in the Caribbean. I had never been there and was excited to go ashore. The night before at the 8:00 p.m. meeting, however, the chief engineer told all officers that they were not going ashore if they do not have the Personnel Qualification Standard (PQS) books updated before pulling in. This required a great deal of work, and I ended up missing liberty because I was holed up doing the updating. When the liberty boat returned to the ship, I saw the chief engineer disembarking, followed by the other division officers.

I asked how they could have updated their books so quickly and discovered that they had not. They just neglected the order, figuring that it was unenforceable. To this day, over thirty years later, I still remember the reason why I missed my opportunity to visit the island. But what made an impression on me was that a leader gave me an order without considering how it might affect me.

There is a saying: A hammer forgets quicker than the nail. I was the nail, and that order is still clear in my mind.

Leaders must always consider the effect their orders have on their people. Sometimes, leaders are not even conscious how much power they possess and the long-term effect of their decisions. Years later, when I became a leadership instructor for all Navy commanding officers going to command positions, I would remind them of the influence they had on their people. I would say, "It is almost criminal how much power and influence you have. You will not even realize every aspect of the impact of your decisions, but you need to be aware of unintended consequences."

One of my captain mentors, Dan Holloway, would later become second fleet commander, and he told me that when I get to command, compare my crew to a water skier behind the boat and me to the boat driver. Any capricious turn may be a lot of fun. But at times, look at the skier behind you trying to hang on.

Leaders learn from all types of other leaders, even those who work for them.

For instance, Chief Evans in my division was young but highly focused. He would not just order the work done; he would also be down in the boiler room using his expertise to solve problems. He would become chief engineer in a larger amphibious ship and our paths would cross again many years later.

Rising Above Bias, Navigating the Black Sea

When the captain gave me my end-of-the-year fitness report, I had quite a few As and a sprinkle of Bs. I thought I was doing pretty good. Then my roommate left his fitness report on his desk and my eyes happen to look at his grades and they were all As. I wondered about that a bit, because I knew I was putting in as many hours as he was. I went to my mentor, Lieutenant Commander (LCDR) Tom Daniel, and explained the situation. He invited me to go to a meeting of African American naval officers with him. That was my first encounter with the National Naval Officers Association (NNOA). I met quite a few Black officers there, and I heard similar stories to my own. Before, I wasn't convinced that I was the victim of racial discrimination when I failed to pass my first EOOW board. Now, though, when other Black officers shared their stories about bias, I began to see a disturbing pattern. I decided that I would investigate the issue and attempt to understand the unspoken, and at times, unconscious effect of racial discrimination in America. I wanted to get to the root cause without creating problem with my friends. I wanted to help them see the light. Because I had a strongly held belief that I was as American as every other American.

Shortly after my wife and I had another child, our ship embarked on a six-month deployment to the Mediterranean. Prior to our departure, Atlantic Fleet Commander Admiral Frank Kelso came to the ship and talked to our officers. He was a four-star flag officer, and the significance of his presence on the ship wasn't lost on any of us. The year before while on deployment, one of our US ships was bumped by a Russian warship while in the Black Sea. We were about to execute that same mission to keep the sea lines of communications free, a core mission for which we had been training.

Shortly thereafter, we got underway with one short blast on the horn. I went back down below and changed my mental focus to an underway mindset. We departed as part of the John F Kennedy Carrier Battle Group, and it would take us ten days to cross the ocean and reach our destination.

I was assigned to the EOOW section in the engineering plant. I thoroughly enjoyed that watch, compared to all other shipboard watches that I would be standing later. The engineer has a certain amount of autonomy not found in other watches. I was the grand master of my plant and my watch. I knew my people and my responsibilities inside and out. My orders were instantly and unquestionably obeyed. Due to my detailed knowledge about every single valve and piece of equipment, I was comfortable with the duty. One time I was in my stateroom and heard a sound that was unfamiliar to me. Something was emitting a lower tone than it should have been. I listened to it carefully and went down to the Aft Fireroom. I walked around the plant and picked up that same low, tonal vibration. Then I found it – again a chattering valve. I told my chief about it and he said yes, the valve was going bad and had it fixed.

Again, it pays to sweat the small stuff. Small problems become big ones if you don't address them early. Leaders need to take responsibility for identifying a seemingly minor glitch that has the potential to turn into a crisis.

We arrived at our destination – our first port was in Villefranche near Monaco. After some sightseeing and receptions, I met some people at one reception that reinforced my optimistic view of humankind. I befriended the son of a Swedish architect by speaking French and English to him, and his father asked me to come and have dinner with them the next day. They had a house overlooking Cannes with a magnificent view, and I had a wonderful dinner with them and stayed overnight. Though they had things to do the next day, they gave me their BMW to drive around, told me to relax in their beautiful house and feel free to partake of the abundant food and wine they had there. They were people who could completely trust another human being with no strings attached. I found myself increasingly confident in and trusting of other people. I decided that most people are good or want to be good, although obstacles sometimes get in the way of this goal.

Back on the ship, we executed our freedom of navigation exercise in the Black Sea, and when we arrived, two Russian ships were waiting for us. They apparently knew we were coming and welcomed us to the Black Sea; they told us that they would accompany us the whole time we were there. We navigated the waters for a few days and then, without any major issue, exited. The Russians thought of the Black Sea as their backyard. Not too many Navies or ships are bold enough to go to their backyard, refusing to be bullied. Back then, we Americans were the only ones who would directly challenge their claim. No overt hostile actions occurred, but they clearly didn't like our intrusion into what they perceived as their territory, and it was a tense situation during the time we were doing our exercise.

Evolving Under a New Leader

We experienced a major ship change when our captain was relieved by Captain Grant D. Fulkerson. The old captain rarely left his cabin and generally wasn't with us on deployment. When he was around, he refrained from any significant interactions with his officers.

When Captain Fulkerson was touring my area of the ship, he asked me about myself, which was the very first time any senior officer onboard the ship has ever inquired about how I was doing. He also asked how come I was a lieutenant and did not have a

SWO pin. I told him I have been in the hole since I had arrived. Captain Fulkerson said he would investigate the possibility of getting me to stand some watches in Combat Information Center (CIC) and the bridge. I was excited about this possibility, because I had assumed it wasn't possible. I had asked the chief engineer about these watches, and he blew me off. The prospect of getting some fresh air and fresh experience during watches was energizing. Good leaders provide their people with opportunities for learning and advancement, and in a very short period of time, Captain Fulkerson did both.

To advance into more senior leadership positions in the Navy is a process that's somewhat different from advancement in business organizations; let me share my experience from this time. It takes about two years to promote from ensign to lieutenant junior grade. Because I spent two years in aviation from 1985 to 1987, I was promoted to LTJG as a matter of routine when I boarded the Biddle. Many LTJGs didn't have their SWO pins, but most LTs did. Because I was now a LT, I was embarrassed by this situation. Though Captain Fulkerson had said he would see about getting me the opportunity to stand watches on CIC and the bridge, that had not happened yet, which meant I had to wait for my SWO pin.

But I went to the Navy Exchange, bought myself a SWO pin, and taped it on my light fixture on top of my bunk, so I could see it every night when I went to sleep. I wanted to remind myself that I needed to go to the bridge and combat some day, and qualify as officer of the deck when we were at sea and as CIC watch officer. More than a reminder, that pin served as motivation to achieve a goal that so far had been out of reach.

Chapter 5

Running the Combat Systems Team

Returning from deployment is a big deal in the Navy, and we were returning after six months away from home. When I arrived, I got to see my newborn Charles who was only a 1-month-old when I departed. As wonderful as it was to see my family again, I had to start training shortly after I arrived home.

Training in the Navy never stops, and it provides a competitive edge in the military as well as in business. People may grouse about having to go through yet another training protocol, but leaders who pay attention to training give their organizations a significant advantage.

A lot of our Navy training involved preparing for every type of scenario involving enemies and how they might strike us. I was assigned watch in the Combat Information Center, and I was so excited about this training assignment that I read and memorized much of the Combat System Doctrine and the CIC Doctrine. I tackled it like the EOOW watch. These combat systems were fascinating and complex. I learned about the SPS-48 E radar, then the Combat Direction System and SYS-2, the system integrator. I took my CIC board and passed.

I also demonstrated what I had learned during a training exercise at sea. We had to turn the ship thirty degrees while hooked up to the other ship. The captain discussed the plan with me, and I executed this complex maneuver. I was able to do this not just because I had studied hard but because my captain had great confidence in his officers – a leadership quality that I'd emulate over the years. One time, we were pulling into Rosy Roads in Puerto Rico. He asked me to go port side to the pier with no tug. Given that I had studied that maneuver, I was able to do the maneuver by the book. I was gaining confidence in my driving abilities. I took the Officer of the Deck (OOD) Underway Board and passed. Now the only hurdle left was my SWO board. I studied very hard for the board and finally obtained my coveted Surface Warfare Officer pin. It took me longer than most people who received it as an ensign or a JG but better late than never.

I was enjoying being on the bridge driving the ship and being the officer responsible for the day's routine, the safety of the crew, and running the ship as an OOD underway.

Bad Boss, Good Boss

Every leader can recall an instance when they worked for someone who was mediocre at best, cruel at worst. Though most of my commanding officers were excellent, I had a few who disappointed me. At the time, it was difficult to accept. With hindsight, however, their behaviors taught me valuable lessons about leadership mistakes and how to avoid them.

One late evening, I had the 2000 to 2400 watch. We had a fire pump in the fireroom that was down for repair. We had ordered the part under an emergency system where it came to us by helicopter. The chief engineer sent a messenger to the bridge to tell me that the part was in, and I needed to write the message to correct the discrepancy to the Navy as soon as I came off watch at midnight. The protocol was to take this message to the captain immediately and communicate to everyone that the product had been received and the repair made. I asked my folks if they had installed the pump and tested it, and they answered no. I found it unwise to tell the world the pump was fixed when we had not yet made sure it was.

Immediately after my watch, I went to see the chief engineer and explained why I hadn't done what he expected me to do. He let loose a string of curse words and called me lazy, accusing me of not wanting to write the report that night. As a result, I deferred to the chief engineer and wrote the report. I took the message to him; he initialed it, and the XO signed it early in the morning. As soon as the captain was up, I took it to him, and he released it.

Shortly thereafter, my guys took the part out of the container and started to install it, but they discovered that they had been shipped the wrong part. I informed the chief engineer of the mistake. The only thing to do was reorder the part.

We could have just sent an update for the right part, if we had not sent the casualty correction message. It was more work for me, but I had no problem doing it. I took it to the chief engineer, then to the XO, and then to the captain. When I told the old man that we had to reorder the same part, he asked me why. I told him that we received the wrong part last night. He ordered me to go and get the chief engineer, so I did. When the captain asked him the same question, his response devastated me. He told the captain that he did not know it was the wrong part and that the division officer (me) insisted on sending the message to correct the discrepancy. The captain ordered the engineer out of the cabin and ordered me to stay. The CO proceeded to give me a wire brush – a harsh verbal critique – that I would never forget.

I retreated to my stateroom and cried. They were not tears of fear nor tears of guilt or shame. They were tears of betrayal. I could not believe that my superior officer could act in such a low manner; I was stupefied. I was disappointed. From then on, I lost all respect for the chief engineer. Nothing he did from that point on would change my opinion.

He had committed a cardinal leadership sin — he had not only lied, but he had failed to support one of his officers who in this instance, deserved his support. I vowed never to make that mistake with anyone who was under my command.

Fortunately, not long after, I was transferred to another department. I went to Combat System, and my new boss was an old, crusty limited duty officer (LDO) lieutenant who I liked a lot. I oversaw the computer system that ran the combat system. It was a highly technical division, and my guys needed only minimum supervision. My boss did not scream at me or curse constantly. One day, we had a piece of gear that broke down. My guys could not fix it, and we had to ask for technical assistance. The expert came in, and I welcomed him aboard and stayed with him as he repaired the equipment. I was asking questions trying to understand what went wrong. I was surprised when he told me that this was the very first time he had an officer tag along with him and ask questions. It validated that I was doing the right thing, and it was a product of my engineering training below deck. I had to be with the guys, not only to know what was going on, but to keep current. I could best understand if I was there to see situations in person.

I was fascinated by the computer that ran the combat system, the UYK-43. It was a mainframe computer that had a redundant system, two computer processing units (CPUs), two memory banks, two of everything. My third-class petty officers knew that computer inside and out, but I never quite mastered it like I mastered the equipment down in the plant. I realized that topsiders do not have a training program as rigorous as the engineers.

Around this time, I had a conversation with my chief that still resonates with me. He said, "You know, sir, you're a good officer. I could have been an officer as well if I had listened to my dad." I asked him what he meant. He said, "After high school, I got tired of studying and found a menial job while staying at home. My dad encouraged me to do something with my life, but I ignored him. Eventually, I moved out and joined the Navy as an enlisted man.

But if my dad had been a bit tougher with me and used his size 10 boot on my behind when I was ignoring him or being disrespectful, I might have gone to college and become an officer."

I would tell this story to my boys, so they understood my willingness to use my size 10 on their derrieres if they messed up. I did not want them to say that I did not give them my best shot.

Thinking about it, this is the same philosophy to which the best bosses subscribe. They aren't mean or discipline people because they enjoy exercising their authority. Instead, they use discipline as a corrective, to nudge people onto the right path.

A Range of Experience

Being an officer on a ship exposes you to myriad situations. Some of these situations have nothing to do with the training you're going through, but they're beneficial nonetheless, because they prepare you to deal with just about anything. When our ship returned to the Caribbean for more training, we received a call one night about a possible drug boat. I was on watch in CIC and got excited about the prospect of catching a bad guy. We found them and boarded the boat in the early morning but discovered nothing in it. Intelligence, however, told us that they were carrying some type of drug merchandise. I came up with a search pattern for another search team to follow. After I sent them on that vector, they captured the bad guys and found $4 million worth of pure cocaine in the very bottom of the boat. The captain gave me credit for the that drug bust and put it in my official record.

We stayed at Puerto Rico's Roosevelt Roads Naval Base – everyone referred to it as Rosy Roads – for an overnight. The XO had put out liberty call for on base only. Seven of the officers went to the officer club and it was closed. One of the officers suggested going to Papa Joe, a club near the back gate so close to the base it was almost universally considered to be on base. We arrived and found there was food and nearly half the ship's crew. Next day, XO found out the crew had left the base and asked all the officers who were at Papa Joe to report to him. As punishment, the next time we were at Rosy Roads, we were confined to the fantail of the ship. This punishment was illegal, because only the captain can restrict an officer on the ship, and it required a lot of paperwork. But the XO's unofficial method communicated to us that we had done wrong but in a way that wasn't entered onto our records.

I had been on the USS Biddle for three years, and though I had received training in many different areas, I had been typecast as a chief engineer. My qualification as an EOOW on a 1,200-pound steam ship seemed to preordain my path. Nonetheless, I was eager to explore other options. As I approached my rotation time, the Navy career counselor and I took a trip to Washington, D.C., to visit our detailers – the people responsible for our assignments. I met with my detailer, and he pulled out my record and I told him I would like to do another ship tour. He told me he had something in the west if I was interested. I said how far west, he said California, I said that sounded good. When he saw my flexibility to go west, he added that he had something even farther west if I was willing to relocate. I asked where, and he said Hawaii. I was exhilarated. I said sign me up.

The USS Biddle left port without me. I had an interim period before reporting to Hawaii, and I was irked that the captain and XO of the ship seemed to think that I was going to take advantage of the situation and not do anything until I had to report. In fact, I was already doing work for the squadron, even though my department head told me I didn't have to come in or work all day. My conscience and work ethic, however, wouldn't let me slack off. I realized that deep within myself, I had a good work habit, that it was intrinsic rather than extrinsic – I didn't need to have a master screaming and barking orders on what I needed to do with four letter-words to get a job done well.

I completed my duties and detached from the USS Biddle (CG 34) in July 1990, as a competent and confident ship driver, a fully qualified EOOW, and a command duty officer (CDO). It was a hard three years but well worth it, because it prepared me well for a successful career in the Navy. I was to report, as a missile officer, to my second ship in November of the same year after attending a few schools.

I enjoyed getting into the basics of missile design and performance. Given that I was already qualified in those systems, I was able to do a deep dive and learn the systems inside and out. For instance, I mastered the Combat Direction System (CDS), the set of computer programs that control the combat system aboard an NTU ship. I went to another school where I learned the Weapon Control System (WCS), the program that controls the weapon system onboard.

While in San Diego attending missile system training, I met an officer who was also taking these courses, and he introduced me to his father who had been a CO before retiring. I had a chance to talk with him about command, and our conversation yielded a valuable leadership lesson. I asked him if there was anything he would do differently, and he said that he was too soft when he was CO. If he had to do it all over again, he told me he would start his command tour as a hard CO, and then relax when necessary. He said it was much easier to start hard and relax later than to go from soft to hard. If you start as an easy captain, the crew gets comfortable with this demeanor; later, if you become tougher, they will struggle with this new persona – they'll feel like you weren't being honest.

I took his lesson to heart because in my experience it made great sense. You make it clear that you have high standards, that you don't tolerate sloppiness or laziness, but over time you gradually reveal your compassion and sense of humor while still maintaining your high standards.

Two Years on the Reeves

I met the USS Reeves in November 1990 at the pier, watching her pull into Hawaii's Pearl Harbor. She was coming in from Japan as a forward-deployed ship. I would learn later that during an exercise an F-18 had mistakenly dropped a bomb on its forecastle.

Fortunately, there were no casualties. Once the ship arrived, it went straight to the shipyard. I then had a chance to help the crew move it off to a barge and drydock the ship.

The next few months were a blur of activity: ripping the old combat system apart to make room for the new one; serving as the electronic readiness officer in the Combat System Department. It was my first time in charge of other officers, and I took it very seriously. I would meet with them every day after quarters to get the status of their division. I would track the status of my parts like a hawk, I needed to know the status of each ordered part and when they would be onboard. Once a week, I would sit with each division officer (DIVO) and his chief, and we would go through these pages of documents in excruciating detail. It kept the officers on their toes and got them ready for the meeting. They knew I would ask them directly about progress, issues, parts, and so forth. At times, I would have them take me to the location to see the actual part and see who was working on it. There is no substitute for management by walking around. I possessed superior knowledge about the status of the gear because I viewed it myself. Once a week, I also walked each single space with the division officer. I encouraged my officers and divisions to maintain custody and ownership of their spaces during the yard period. It is easy to surrender the space to the shipyard and assume they will keep everything clean and safe; that was not always the case.

I was also the ship's safety officer, and in that capacity, I brought copies of my safety discrepancy reports to the department heads, the XO and the CO, Captain David McKenzie. The CO was an easy person to talk to and work with and each department head had access to him. He set the tone for a friendly working environment. Once a month, we would gather at his house to either hail or farewell shipmates, whether anyone was coming or leaving.

Personally, I and my family loved our time in Hawaii, the islands' wonderful environment mirroring that of the ship. From walking on the beautiful beaches with my wife to coaching my sons' soccer teams, it was paradise.

Everything was working out professionally. Our new XO, Commander Andy Tamayo, was one of the best XOs I'd ever had, and he made work a pleasure. I also began working on submitting the ship for a safety award. I studied what past winners had done to get the award and implemented those policies with additional ones. We ended up winning not one but two safety awards, and then we won a prestigious third one. Upon receipt of the Green S award from the Admiral. Captain McKenzie stated in front of the crew that the credit belongs to the safety officer, who relentlessly went after every safety discrepancy onboard the ship and ensured they were corrected. This was one of my proudest moments in the Navy to date.

Hard work often pays off, not just in results but rewards.

Captain McKenzie departed, and a new CO came a board. As I've noted, Captain McKenzie was a genuinely nice guy who fostered a friendly environment. The pace was about to change, however.

The new CO turned out to be a high-speed, low-drag kind of captain. We all had to fasten our seatbelts and prepare for an adrenaline-fueled ride. We welcomed aboard Captain Peter A. C. Long. Captain Long was the kind of person who filled the room with energy once he walked in. You could see it in his eyes, in his behavior – you could see his mind spinning fast. He had very high expectations for the people working for him, and he expected them to know their job, their people, and their spaces.

At the weekly shipyard status meeting in the shipyard conference room, the CO would gather all his department heads and other key personnel; I was there as the safety officer. Though the chief engineer was always on top of his game and knew the status of all the critical paths, other department heads were called to the carpet when they couldn't explain to the CO why certain jobs were delayed. The new CO started to put pressure on them to up their games.

The pressure had gotten to my boss, who said that he'd been on Tylenol and Maalox for the last few weeks to deal with the stress. A few days later, he walked to the CO's cabin and tendered his resignation; he was immediately transferred off the ship. The CO told Mike (my fellow officer) to keep working with the other half of the department. My three divisions were running smoothly, and my three division officers knew the status of every job in the division. Additionally, they were briefing me on the status of every job just like the chief engineer was doing for his divisions. I knew this method worked, because every week I saw the engineer shoot out his status to the CO the instant he asked for it. It was really a question of accountability – holding your division officers responsible – and also of training – training your division officers on what to look for, to inspect, and on what to brief you. Also, as a department head, I had to be interested and involved in what was transpiring.

Facing a Tough Challenge

We had a final inspection scheduled in a few weeks, and the team lead from Combat System's inspection team told the CO there was no way we would be ready for the final inspection: The missile magazines were not up to snuff. I'd noted this issue in my safety inspection reports, but they hadn't been addressed aggressively. I knew where the problems resided, but as safety inspector I wasn't able to correct them.

For this reason, I went to the CO and asked him to switch me and Mike. Mike had another major collateral duty that was taking a lot of his time away from his group, and my group was running like clockwork and would be easy for Mike to take over. The CO told me to make the switch effective immediately.

A lot of leaders delay this type of decision. They think on it, form a committee to analyze it, then brainstorm options. Sometimes, this can be a useful strategy. Other times, immediate action must be taken, and the best leaders know when to act fast. The CO knew.

I did the swap with Mike and gathered the leadership of the Battery Control Organization in the Combat System Maintenance

Center. I told them that we had little time, so we needed to double our work pace. I also identified the most problematic area: The Third Division Missile System had an excellent officer running it, but his group needed direction and focus and was the target of the inspector's worries. Like the CO, I made a quick decision: I swapped the job of two officers. LT Jojo San Miguel was an engineer who knew what to do to get his new division under control, and I had full confidence in him. My direction to him was to work it, brief me daily, and let me know where and when he needs assistance. I added that my oversight on him would be minimum, but I was here for him anytime and anywhere he needed me. I also marshalled the support of other officers, including ones on other ships, such as LCDR Chuck Neary, a CSO onboard another cruiser in Hawaii, the USS Worden. We had gone to Combat System School together in Dam Neck before reporting aboard. I went to see him, and he offered his full support for whatever I needed.

Leaders are made or broken on assignments such as this one, where they're trying to achieve stretch goals with tight deadlines.

I began by sitting with the missile officer and all his chiefs, compiling a list of discrepancies involving the inspector's reports, my safety discrepancy reports, and various other reports. We consolidated these lists into a single discrepancy report and assigned each of them a number and a priority. By establishing a system of accountability, we began making progress on the fixes. This system required that I possess the power to hire or to fire – the CO never explicitly gave me this power, but implicitly his command to "fix it" meant I could do whatever needed to be done.

I would go with the CO to shipyard meetings and was able to state the status of every single combat system job in that the yard would bring up. If the yard told the CO that a combat system part in was being delayed, then I would raise my hand and explain that the part was in Mechanicsburg, Pennsylvania, with a shipment date of two days ago, and that I expected it to arrive no later than Monday. To ensure that there was follow through and the part arrived and was installed, I made sure that up and down the line everyone was accountable to another person, cascading down from me and ascending upward from the lowest-ranking Navy man.

I dove 100 percent into my work and did not look back. I would be on the job by 0600 and would sometimes catch the last shuttle boat at 2300 at night. Nidda understood what I was facing and was 100 percent behind me. Not everyone under my command was similarly understanding. I started receiving nasty phone calls at home and menacing silences and hang ups on my private line. Once, Nidda saw someone loitering around the house – it could have been a random person or any angry seaman wanting to scare us. I was asking a lot of my people, and at least one person resented it. But I was undeterred. More to the point, I was focused on the finish line.

Good leaders sometimes need to do end runs around established protocols.

I would go with the missile chief to the ship graveyard, and with the graveyard supervisor's permission, we would salvage some parts that we needed; we had learned that some of the systems onboard those ships were still functional, and we could use them to bring our missile fire suppressant system back online. When I ordered a part and it could not come in on time, I would go to Chuck Neary on the USS Worden and he would give me the what I needed, then I would pay him back when mine arrived. One time, he needed a first-class expert for something, and I sent him the individual he needed.

We finally put the missile fire suppressant system back together just before the inspectors arrived. They would give us the thumbs up or down on our repair. We all knew the status of the jobs, and we tested them to the best of our abilities. What we did not know is whether once we put it all together if it would work, and we were not allowed to place the full system in operation until the inspectors arrived.

The captain trusted me as an officer, and his trust helped me grow as a leader. One day, I served as the command duty officer

(CDO) and the ship had to do a dead stick move from one berth to another. The captain had a meeting off the ship at the same time. He told me as CDO to take charge of the move with the pilot. Usually when a ship moves, there's a lot of commotion. This time there was not. I briefed my watch team and set a modified sea detail and went to the bridge. We performed the move flawlessly! When the captain returned, the ship was in a new berth. Captain Long was a confident ship driver and leader and was not afraid to trust his officers and give them the chance to lead.

When the inspection experts arrived, and I took the team leader to the missile magazines, and he was floored. He went to the CO and stated what he'd seen was beyond belief. He told the CO we were ready to load missiles and commence preparation for the, Combat System Ship Qualification Test (CSSQT). Our hard work had paid off.

We had two missile-firing teams: a Blue and Gold team. I was the tactical action officer (TAO) for the Blue team, and the Ops Officer LCDR Doug Lowry was the TAO for the Gold team. We started training as a team for the missile firings by first going through the firing checklist with everyone performing their functions.

Around this time, the captain received an invitation for a special briefing. The newest Navy destroyer was being built in Bath Iron Works in Maine. Commander (CDR) John Morgan and his combat system officer (CSO) were in Hawaii to brief leadership about the capabilities of this first-class destroyer, USS Arleigh Burke (DDG 51). We had been hearing about this ship's awesome capabilities and now I was going to have a chance to meet its captain, as Captain Long invited me and a few other officers to accompany him. The USS Arleigh Burke was be the newest warship in the US fleet and the most powerful destroyer in the history of naval warfare. (I couldn't imagine that one day I would be the ninth commanding officer of the USS Arleigh Burke.

At the time, I was concentrating on leading one of the largest departments onboard the ship. We accelerated the pace of preparation for the final missile shots to test the brand-new NTU system we had just installed. I would spend many hours motivating the crew or learning by watching them as they got everything ready. I would focus on the actual combat system during the day, and on the administrative aspect of work in the afternoon and evenings. I was probably an inefficient way of doing the work but necessary – I had not yet been to Department Head School where they would supposedly teach me the tricks of the trade. Fortunately, I was on the list to attend after I completed this tour. The CO and XO offered me the opportunity to take the Command Qualification test that was delivered for the officer who had resigned, which meant that in addition to all my other duties, I had to study for it a few hours daily. My counterpart on the USS Worden, LCDR Chuck Neary, had already passed the test and offered me invaluable assistance studying for the test. He helped me grasp the threat matrix and know the weapons and tactics of potential enemy navies.

Like many leaders, I had an extra-large capacity for work, but that capacity was rapidly being exhausted with my mounting responsibilities. Fortunately, I was surrounded by people who made all my tasks a bit easier.

You can learn a huge amount from a good boss, and my CO was excellent. I respected him, of course, but I also enjoyed our conversations – on more than one occasion, I asked him what he was thinking about. Perhaps this boldness from a junior officer puzzled him, but I believe he saw that I was hungry to understand how leadership worked, and he was willing to show me and be my mentor.

Leadership can be lonely, as I was discovering. Normally, as I enjoyed the camaraderie of being with other division officers, but I was cut off from this camaraderie by my position. Grousing about leadership, a favorite wardroom activity, wasn't possible because I would be complaining about myself (and the XO and CO). No doubt, the division officers and the chiefs must have talked about me and how prickly or inconsiderate I was and how hard I was working them. But because I was so intent on making things happen, I didn't dwell on their opinions of me.

I was standing my watch as CDO and did my round of the ship after eight o'clock report, which was held at 1900. It was always a favorite joke around the Navy when the duty section chief would call the CDO and ask, "At what time would the 8 o'clock report be taken today?" The report is called the "8 o'clock report"; back in the olden days, it must have been taken at 8 o'clock p.m. The report maintained its name of the 8 o'clock report, but it has nothing to do with taking it then. It is one of the fine Navy traditions. Sometimes, the name of something does not particularly match its function. Nonetheless, the tradition was still maintained. It may not make sense for any landlubbers but for us seagoing dogs, these traditions have meaning.

One of my CDO duty days, I dreamed that I was standing on an island and looking eastward. Then I saw a huge ship coming from left to right. I had never seen a ship that big before in my life. In the dream, I started thinking to myself, *This is my ship, this is the ship where I will be the Captain.* I noticed that that ship that I thought was so big was actually only a tug pulling an even bigger ship. Compared to the ship that the tug was pulling in size, the tug was nothing. Then another thought entered my dreaming mind: *The biggest ship you thought was yours was only a tug towing your real ship. The ship that is being towed is your ship.*

When I awoke, I didn't dismiss the dream. I've had weird dreams and presentiments since I was a child, and several times they've had significance in real life.

Lessons about leadership can come from unexpected places at unexpected times — it's not always through training or formal feedback from a boss or solving a problem at work.

We were on the ship passing Kauai, and I was the officer on duty when the CO came to the bridge. We stood there watching the beautiful beaches and coastline of that beautiful island. We did not say anything to each other for a while. Then I made a comment about the island's natural beauty, and this was the first time the CO responded to me as a person rather than as a CO. We then started talking about the future and Captain Long told me about his desire to teach after he retired, that he would enjoy being a schoolteacher. We then stood silently for another few minutes, soaking in the beauty of the land we were sailing past. It was one of the moments at sea that I will cherish forever – a simple conversation with my commanding officer on the bridge of a US warship at sea.

Best Shot

The day finally arrived to test our new $64 million missile system. We were off the coast of Kauai at Barking Sands, Hawaii, early in the morning. The water was calm, and it was a beautiful, sunshiny day. When I came to the Combat Information Center, my blue team had already manned up. I sat on the TAO chair and conducted a radio check with my watch team; communications were good. I said a few words of encouragement – that this was the day we had all been waiting for, let's be on our game and do it the way we have been trained. The CO walked in, and I gave him a brief of the situation. Radio communications with the shore declared that they would start the countdown in five minutes.

The CO was in a particularly good mood. He wanted to set the world record for this type of missile shoot. The record was currently held by another NTU ship, and my team knew exactly what to do to beat it. Then the countdown to launching the drone started, and once it was launched, we had permission to kill it upon detection within the missile envelope. We picked up the drone on our search radars. Upon receiving a recommend fire from the fire control system, I gave permission to fire, and it zoomed upward with an unmistakable whoosh – I heard and felt the beautiful sound of the SM-2 leaving the launcher. The target was destroyed within seconds. Although we didn't set the record, we completed the exercise and were certified to use the system.

My deployment was scheduled for May 1992, and I was told to report to Newport for Department Head School starting in May. I continued to lead the department while standing my CDO watches. My relief, LCDR Glen Sears, would not arrive until after I departed the ship. I accelerated the pace of my study, and I began taking the Command-at-Sea written test the ship had ordered for the previous department head while we were off the coast of Honolulu. My expectation was that it would be a nice and calm day at sea. The XO gave me permission to use the embarked group commander's cabin to take the test. The day, though, turned out not to be as calm as usual. The ship was rocking, and the seas were a bit rough. I went to the cabin and took the eight-hour test. I got a bit seasick as I took the test and my stomach was churning, but I hung in there and answered the questions to the best of my ability. I finished it and returned it to the XO.

The time came for me to leave the ship. I enjoyed my tour on the USS Reeves (CG 24), challenging though it was. It validated the American dream for me – if you work hard and perform well, your effort will be rewarded.

Chapter 6

Four Commanding Officers: Learning to Work for and Learn from Very Different Leaders

In May of 1992, I moved to Newport and started Department Head School. I had passed the Command-at-Sea test on the USS Reeves as a second tour division officer. Department Head School was great, providing instruction in all the shipboard programs for which a department head is responsible. The first tactical course was Anti-Submarine Warfare (ASW) taught by a previous XO of the Submarine USS Miami. It was a great ASW course, and for the first time I understood that warfare from the perspective of a warrior who has been there and done that. He got into the nitty gritty details of the science of detecting and killing an enemy ship or another submarine.

We also learned about the fast and exciting world of Anti-Air Warfare (AAW). It was the very opposite of ASW (also known as awfully-slow-warfare). ASW requires a lot of thinking and the ability to play a cat and mouse game. AAW demands speed. It is the world of supersonic aircraft and missiles coming to kill your ship at the speed-of-sound reaction time. If you do not know your techniques, tactics, and procedures (TTPs) before the attack, you're in a world of trouble when the attack commences.

Mastering AAW and ASW represents a common leadership task. The ability to master two opposing processes is crucial, in that throughout a career, heads of organizations must be adept at two tasks that are diametrically opposed – running the organization effectively under severe budget constraints and spending aggressively while pursuing a growth strategy, for instance. Given the volatile world in which we live and work, this ability to master opposing strategies is essential for situational leadership.

We also studied Surface Warfare – the art of killing another ship – and Strike Warfare – how to use Tomahawk missiles for land attacks. Then we took the final TAO exam and were assigned ships. I was assigned to the USS Sides, a warship docked in San Diego.

Leading Large Groups

I reported to the USS Sides in January 1993, and met the CO, the XO, and others, and I was excited about overseeing my department. This department had three officers and fifty technicians. Before I had a master chief, two chiefs, and over forty-five boiler technicians, and on my second tour, I oversaw eight other officers and a department of over a hundred. I was becoming confident in my ability to lead large groups.

The new challenge involved the ship's mission. USS Sides was a reserve ship and thus, assigned as primary mission to train the reserves. It was a mission that I enjoyed. However, the Navy clearly expected us to operate as a training platform for the reserves, but we were also expected to operate as well as an active-duty ship. As important as training the reserves was, these individuals were still focusing on their civilian jobs so we only were able to work them once a month. They arrived Friday evening after completing their "real" jobs, and we would get underway on Saturday and return on Sunday late morning. They would go home, and we would turn around on Monday and get underway again for regular fleet operations. Thus, we didn't have much time to train the reserves to the point that they could perform effectively.

This is not an unusual leadership challenge – to be given a mission and lack the time or other resources to accomplish it in an ideal manner.

It's also not unusual that young leaders must transition from one boss to another. When I started on the USS Sides, our captain was maniacal about responding quickly to any communication. When underway, he expected us to answer radio calls immediately over our communication systems. I managed to do what he wanted by dedicating a watch personnel to monitor communications – not the best use of personnel. On other ship types, this is a normal process because every watch stander is on a headset, but frigates were a bit different. The CO would shoot out of his cabin fuming when anyone failed to answer immediately on a radio call.

A Change of Command: From Bad to Worse

At first, I was heartened when a new CO came on board to replace the old one; he appeared to be a nice guy. He was a reserve officer, the very first and only one for whom I would have had the pleasure of working. I had a major combat system inspection, Combat System Readiness Review (CSRR). We prepared very well for that inspection. I had periodic sessions with my division officers, reviewing their entire work package and equipment status and ensured every discrepancy was documented. I treated it like our last major combat system inspection on the ship. I invited the CO to come give a welcome aboard remark and that inspection went smoothly. But at the end, the captain made a comment that troubled me a bit. He alluded to the fact that I ran the inspection as if I was the one in charge of the event. It puzzled me. After all, I was in charge of my department, why shouldn't I act like it? I decided I wouldn't let his comment bother me. I assumed that I had misunderstood the CO's comment.

Our deployment was for forty-five days in the Pacific Ocean off the coast of South America. The operation officer Ops and I were standing the TAO Watch port and starboard. We would spend the entire deployment in this situation. I would have the watch from 0600 to 1200, and he would take it from 1200 to 1800. Then I would come back on from 1800 to 2400, and he would take it from 2400 to 0600. I was afforded three or four hours of sleep a night, but the Ops officer was pushing his limit working all day and waking up at 2300 the night before to get ready to relieve me on the hour. Ops should have gone to bed to rest up before coming to relieve me at midnight. Instead, the XO expected him to be at his eight o'clock report meeting before going to brief the CO, usually before bedtime at 2000. Ops would only go to bed between 2000 and 2300. That was not enough sleep on which to function properly.

One day, I stood my regular 1800 to 2400 watch and Ops came up to relieve me at midnight. He was so exhausted that I told him to go back to bed for a few more hours and that I would send someone to wake him up around 3:00 a.m., at which time I would take two or three hours break and come back up to relieve him.

Unfortunately, the CO discovered that I was taking the Ops shift, and for the first time since our deployment, he showed up at the CIC and confronted me with his discovery. I explained to him that my shipmate was so tired that I had volunteered to keep the watch for him. The CO flew into a rage, lambasting me in front of the crew. He ordered me to wake up my fellow officer and instruct him to stand his watch. I did so, and the CO then verbally abused the Ops officer.

Later, I apologized to this officer because it was my idea that he grabs some extra sleep, but he was gracious and again thanked me for helping him. I was flabbergasted by the CO's behavior. I thought I was doing something good, but he thought I was eroding his authority by changing a watch bill that he had personally approved.

Once again, I lost respect for the officer in command. He was more concerned about his authority than the welfare of his crew. I found it selfish and conduct unbecoming of an officer of his rank and position. This is where I promised myself that I would look carefully over the watch bill and that, when and if I ever become an XO and CO, I would carefully review it for all unintended effects and consequences on my officers and crew. Dumb policy made by leadership can have devastating effects on those they lead.

We successfully completed that deployment and returned home to San Diego. Then it was the chief engineer's turn to have his inspection, the feared Operational Propulsion Plan Evaluation (OPPE). Usually, each department head is fully responsible for his departmental inspection as I was for mine a few months earlier. The captain appeared worried about this upcoming inspection, especially when the chief engineer called in sick for a few days right before the inspection. I was looking forward to my nephew, Robert Allen, coming to visit and had made plans to take him and my family to Disney on a Saturday.

Up until this point, I had been completely focused on the ship and my responsibilities, and this was the one family event outside of work that I had planned. The engineering inspection was to start on Monday. I had duty on Friday from 0700 until 0700 on Saturday. I was supposed to be relieved by the Ops officer as CDO on Saturday. I spent Friday focusing most of my energy on the engineering plant, having my watch team cleaning and wiping the entire plant as our contribution. Late in the evening, the CO called. I gave him the rundown on the preparation we had been doing. I appreciated that the CO depended on me and my contribution, though I figured the engineering department head was the one the CO was really depending on.

The CO told me that he would come to the ship tomorrow, but I didn't tell him that I was going to Disney the next day. Given that it was my day off and that my department wasn't directly involved in the inspection, I didn't think this would be an issue. In addition, I knew that Ops would come and relieve me and be there for additional inspection preparation; Ops was a nuclear-trained engineer, a much better engineer that I could ever dream of being. Ops came onboard by 0600 on Saturday and relieved me by 0700. I gave him the full turnover and left the ship, going to Disney with the family.

I returned to the ship on Monday, and my department stood ready to help the engineering department if our help was requested or if I found it necessary to do something to help a shipmate. The CO was a bit cold toward me later that day, and I thought it prudent to let him focus on the engineering department. We passed the inspection, but afterward I noticed that the CO continued to be cold toward me. I did not ask him what was wrong – it wasn't my place to question his behavior. I suspected, however, that he must have expected me to be there on Saturday when he arrived and was disappointed that I was absent.

For most of my time onboard, I was the special sea and anchor OOD – the officer in charge of ship handling during special and dangerous situations. I was getting close to the end of my tour and had trained another officer to take my place. I trained him to be my relief as OOD, and eventually turned over the watch to him but stayed in the bridge to monitor his performance. I was there to help him if he needed assistance, but I let him run his watch because one day I would leave the ship, and he would have to stand the watch without me.

My good friend, LCDR Chuck Neary, was my detailer and believed in my qualification and abilities. For this reason, he told me he was going to recommend me as CSO and department head for a brand-new Aegis Destroyer that was being built. A few days later, Chuck called me back and said my nomination has been accepted. Back then, being assigned to the Aegis world under the umbrella of one of the finest organizations in the Navy PMS 400 was an honor reserved for the very best and brightest SWOs. My orders came in and it was time to transfer to Bath, Maine.

First, I was to report in April 1994 in Norfolk for training. Shortly before departing, I went to the captain's cabin to sign my Fitness Report. Normally this event only involves the CO and the officer concerned. I was a bit surprised to see the XO in the room as I went in to sign my final Fitness Report. I sat down and the CO told me that I had "played the role" of being CSO very well. I looked at him and then looked at the XO; I did not know how to interpret his comment. I told him I thought I was the CSO, and that I was not playing a role. He then told me that I took it very well when I got fired as special sea and anchor detail OOD. He said even when he assigned me to bridge safety, I showed up on time and was always professional in my dealings on the bridge.

I maintained my composure and again looked at the XO to judge his reaction; he was as surprised as I was. I then realized that the best way to deal with this situation was to maintain silence and not question the man's authority. Obviously, he had felt very threatened by me as a junior leader on his ship. I didn't mean to usurp his authority, but I must have done something that suggested I was usurping it.

My future resided in the captain's hands. During the next few tension-filled minutes before I signed my final report, I waited to see if the CO would ask the XO to change whatever was in there and give me an adverse report – the type of report that kills careers. I remained silent, refusing to address his absurd statements. He finally handed me my report, which I read very carefully. It was a glowing report, completely at odds with his negative words. I decided to just sign it and get the hell out of Dodge.

Later, I ran into the XO when I was assigned to the Pentagon and went over the events of that day with him. He agreed that the CO acted a bit weird, and that the conversation was not pre-coordinated with him; the CO called him and asked him to be present during the debrief. Since that day, I have never seen the man and don't understand why he said what he did.

Again, however, I've found value in reflecting on negative experiences involving leaders to whom I reported. I tried to put myself in his shoes to see how I would react. What would I do if I expected an officer to be there when I needed him and he was absent? Though I would be disappointed, I would also assess the circumstances and determine if he was to blame – or if I shared some or all of the responsibility.

Your people can't read your mind, no matter how transparent you believe yourself to be.

I never wanted my officers to doubt or misinterpret what I needed. For this reason, I tried to put myself in their shoes, and then tried to communicate as clearly as I could and repeat the message to make sure it got through.

My next assignment came through: Report to the new Navy Destroyer USS Gonzalez (DDG 66) in Bath, Maine.

USS Gonzalez

You can't lead if you're not prepared. Fortunately, the Navy prepared us with great intelligence and effort. Invariably, leaders make mistakes when they're placed in new situations or jobs. If they're prepared, however, they may still make errors, but training usually helps limit the damage.

When I reported to my new assignment in Norfolk, there were only three shipmates already in place. I would be the fourth crew-member, the second officer, and the first highest ranking officer to report. The other three had established an environment of friendliness and caring that would be the hallmark of our ship and the first team aboard. Chief Jones, the tomahawk chief, was the ultimate professional; he was skilled and meticulous with everything he did.

FC3 Hynman was the nicest person on Earth, always willing to do what was best for the ship. He occupied a special place as the very first blue shirt to report aboard. ENS Wyatt would occupy a special place in my book of shipmates. He was an LDO, previously a chief petty officer (CPO), who was dedicated, loyal, and a pleasure with which to work. He would keep me apprised of every aspect of the ship. Together, we transitioned the arriving crew members onto the ship. Fortunately, all four first crewmembers were in assigned to my department.

Then I started training at Chincoteague, Virginia. Classes focused on learning Aegis, and we were taught the console operations of the combat system. Next, I took a course in Dahlgren, Virginia, two hours north of Norfolk, and there I met other crew members. We were given gigantic books about the Aegis weapon system. I would go to class during the daytime, 0800 to 1600, go to grab some dinner, and would return to class to read and study from 1800 until midnight. I had to finish reading the book on SPY, the Aegis radar. I understood then that my success as a TAO in this new ship depended on my thorough understanding of the combat system, especially SPY, the heart of the system. I studied and read that book with great diligence. One day, we had to give a presentation to our CO, Captain Hunt, and he was fascinated as I wrote the equation from memory describing why and how a double missile shot has a much higher probability of kill "Pk" than a single shot. I also took some other shorter classes, such as nuclear safety, drug prevention, and other required training.

As other crewmembers reported, we oriented them and eventually we went to Bath, Maine in September 1993, and began further preparations for the USS Gonzalez. As the first crew of the ship, we had the privilege of putting together our own combat system handbook for the crew. I examined the weapons' handbooks from previous destroyers and compared them with a few cruisers' handbooks as well. Together, my officers and I came up with a comprehensive and well-written handbook. The purpose of the book was to take a newly assigned crewmembers and guide them through all the spaces, showing them all the equipment in the space, and provide an introduction as well to the equipment and a description.

Management by walking around has almost become a cliché in business circles, but good leaders know the value of eyeballing their environments — they make the effort to see their people, processes, and policies in action.

When I and three other crewmembers were the first to arrive in Bath, we decided that we would walk and visit the entire ship by going through at least ten spaces a day. During my time aboard, I walked and crawled in every space on the good USS Gonzalez. I would even enter every single cofferdam and void before final closeout, as if it was some type of final shipboard inspection. It was exciting to see the ship being put together one space at a time. In the first few weeks at Bath, I represented the captain in the weekly production meetings led by retired submarine Captain Roland Melcher. Roland was highly respected and perhaps even a bit feared by the yard engineers and production crew. Any problem that I brought to Roland's attention would be quickly addressed; he was a no-nonsense kind of leader. I liked him and his style a lot; he would not settle for any excuses.

It pays to observe other leaders' styles. As I've noted, you can learn a lot even from bad bosses and make sure you don't commit the same errors. And you can learn even more from leaders you admire.

Around this time, I encountered the CO of USS Carney, CDR Lanny King. His outgoing personality was impressive. He would tell his crew and officers that if life was a choice between being happy and being grumpy, then he opted for happy. I remember him loading his canoe on top of his SUV on a Friday for the weekend. Then, one Monday upon returning from work, we all heard the terrible news. CDR King died over the weekend; the cause was an aneurysm. It was devastating news, and I got to thinking about fragility of life, how he could be with us one day, and the next day be gone forever. I decided to live my life to its fullest every day and to do my utmost every day. Just like Lanny King, if I am given a choice to be happy or to be grumpy, I would choose to be happy, no matter what curve ball life sends my way.

I think this translates into my leadership style. The vast majority of people prefer to work for happy rather than grumpy individuals. They prefer optimistic, upbeat bosses, not doom-and-gloom ones. People work harder and are more engaged when they work for someone with a ready smile and a positive outlook.

As the ship's construction proceeded, I focused on my primary job as department head/CSO and supervising other crew members. I gave our combat systems expert full authority to run the day-to-day operation, allowing me to address the bigger strategic direction of the entire department. The ASW officer, fire control officer, the missile officer, and the gunnery officer reported directly to the weapons officer "Weps" – the supersmart and brilliant LT Mark Vandroff who was a pre-commissioning officer on the USS Arleigh Burke (DDG-51), who together with the system test officer (STO) and the electronic material officer (EMO) reported directly to me. Another duty was as senior watch officer, overseeing officer training, officer development, and officer watch assignments.

I also served as commissioning coordinator, and in this role, I assisted with the commissioning of our ship when it was ready. The crisp and sharp LT Phil Sobeck was my right-hand man in this crucial role. The first official function on the ship was the christening. The next big function was moving from the block to the water. This was a special day in the life of the ship. They started greasing the skids by pumping a special fluid between the ship and the blocks. All preparations were made. Then at the crucial hour, after the speeches, after a bottle of champagne was cracked on the hull by Mrs. Dolia Gonzalez (Freddy's mother), the USS Gonzalez glided down the blocks and made its way into the water for the first time in her life.

Leaders juggle roles and responsibilities, and I learned to keep multiple balls in the air during this time.

Mastering Complexity

The launch of a ship is a complicated affair, requiring coordination of lots of moving parts and people.

It is great preparation for any leader, because whether you're launching a product line, running a startup, or implementing a new program, you must be able to deal effectively with multiple factors.

The ship began a series of trials, designed to test various systems and structures – any discrepancy between how something was supposed to work and how it did work required repairs at the Bath Iron Works. The ship did well, and the motto of the Bath shipyard, "Bath built is best built," was appropriate.

To build a ship from scratch takes a lot of work and a dedicated team of sailors willing to work hard. But most of all, it takes great leadership, and we were lucky to have been under the command of Commander Fred Allard. Finally, the ship was ready for all of us to come aboard.

It was a beautiful day when we all lined up and walked to the ship. We all went to our own spaces onboard the ship; we had our workspaces and our living spaces, everything was in spectacular order. It was a team effort that got us there. We were in-commission special, meaning that we lived onboard the ship but were not yet commissioned, so the ship was still designated as Pre-commissioning Unit Gonzalez (PCU Gonzalez) – she was not yet a "USS" ship, meaning a United States warship ready to fight and win. That would occur during the actual commissioning.

We were excited to be onboard the ship because this is how we would get to know it – all the quirks and other traits that every ship possesses. Once on board, our next event was to move the ship from the yard and head out to be commissioned. I was the first OOD in charge of driving the ship and getting it underway from the shipyard and into open ocean. We passed the Portland lighthouse on our starboard side, and then we entered the open ocean. We made a stop in Norfolk for a few days prior to heading down to Texas; Norfolk would be our homeport. Finally, the day came, we left Norfolk, and were on our way to officially become a commissioned ship.

The commissioning of a US warship is very complex. There are thousands of details that need to be planned. Fortunately, we had a guy who had done tons of these events for the Navy. He had a master list of what needed to happen, from the design of the commissioning brochure to the list of invitees, to guest speakers, to ordering chairs. He gave me a copy of the master checklist, and I created a plan for who should do what.

But planning is only part of the process. Pride is another aspect.

Leaders instill pride. They recognize the value when their people and communities are invested in the enterprise.

To that end, I saw the value of creating and featuring plaques (a Navy tradition) aboard the ship for crew members in recognition of their accomplishments. Unfortunately, the Navy doesn't pay for these plaques.

Fortunately, the town of Edinburgh, Texas, was willing to do so. Our ship was named after Sgt. Alfredo "Freddy" Gonzalez, a hero's hero. Author John Flores wrote a terrific book, *When the River Dreams*, about Gonzalez (and I wrote the foreword), who received the medal of honor for his bravery during the Vietnam war – he was killed during the war after knocking out a key enemy rocket position. He was cherished and loved by the Edinburg, Texas, where his mother, Dolia, still lives and works.

The city decided they wanted to fund the plaques. Under the leadership of Mayor Joe Ochoa, several citizens of Edinburg sponsored a crewmember and donated fifty dollars for a plaque for each sailor. In a sense, each donor adopted the sailor that their plaque went to; I have never seen such pride in the face of a city's residents when we arrived in the city for the commissioning.

To reach Texas, we went south from Virginia, past Florida on the right, made a right into the Gulf of Mexico and sailed straight into Corpus Christi and then, Ingleside, the Navy base where we would be commissioned. Shortly after we entered the Gulf, we received an emergency message: A hurricane was forming ahead of us and if we continued, we would take it head on. The recommendation came from Fleet Headquarters in Norfolk for us to turn around and hang around the Yucatan peninsula for a day or two until the hurricane passed. We followed the recommendation. Then the captain decided to press on to our commissioning place in Texas, so we could adhere to scheduled events.

The plan was to proceed through the tail end of Hurricane Josephine. This may not seem like a particularly difficult task, but in fact, the tail end is as bad as the front end. We were moving at twenty-five knots in order to make up for the lost time. As we got closer and closer to Josephine, the seas were exceptionally rough. We went through twelve to fifteen-foot seas with an occasional eighteen-footer, if not more.

As we moved through the hurricane, I was on the bridge one evening as OOD, and the captain saw me and said, "You and I are the two old sea dogs in this ship; you are still hanging in there and not getting seasick." Over half of the crew was out of commission, miserable on their racks riding the stormy waters. The only other time in my Navy career I remember going through such rough seas was on the USS Biddle as we journeyed from the straits of Messina toward Corsica. Back then, the XO said that if you are not on watch, go to your rack, as it is the safest place you can be over the next few hours as we passed the storm.

Our XO said essentially the same thing to our crew. After my watch, I went straight to my own rack. We rode it, and finally the seas got calmer and soon we were out of it. I then realized how well built these ships were. We knew the limits of the hull, which were designed to ride through a maximum sea, and we did not exceed the limits (though in 18-foot waves, it felt like the ship might break in two); the ship can take much more sea roughness than we humans can.

We arrived in Ingleside, Texas, on Tuesday, I believe, and moored in position port side to the pier for the upcoming commissioning ceremony on Friday. The next day, most of the crew got on busses to visit our namesake hometown of Edinburg, Texas. There was a celebration waiting for us. We all checked in at the Echo Hotel, and Mrs. Gonzalez and the entire contingent were there to greet us. Our first stop was at the Freddy Gonzalez Park, where we planted trees and made hand- or footprints on with our names or initials on a brand-new pavement. Then we visited the Freddy Gonzalez Elementary School. The principal had come to our baptism in Bath, and I remember her very well. She was proud to be principal of the school. The school yearbook included pictures of us with the school children. Later in the afternoon, we all went to a football match between the two rival high schools at the Freddy Gonzalez Stadium. The city of Edinburg is very proud of their Vietnam hero; they are also equally proud of their Hispanic heritage. For the evening, they had events organized for us at Cadillac Jack right across from the Echo hotel. The crew had so much fun just hanging around with people from the town, Mrs. Gonzalez, all her friends, and fans. It was a full day of fun in the city of Freddy. We then headed back to the ship for the final rehearsal on Thursday. We also had a special dinner with all the people in Corpus Christi who volunteered their time and effort to thank them for their full support. And finally, the big day we had all been waiting for arrived, Friday, the day of the commissioning.

As the commissioning coordinator, I double- and triple-checked my list to ensure nothing was left to chance. The actual commissioning ceremony went flawlessly. In attendance were the secretary of the Navy, the senator and congressmen from Texas, the chief of naval operations (CNO), and various other dignitaries. After the ceremony, we left Texas and returned to Norfolk to ready ourselves as a fighting crew.

After this, we left for a major exercise at sea, first pulling into St. Marteen for the weekend and then departing for a gun exercise. During this trip, I started thinking about my career to date: I had spent two years aboard this ship as a second tour department head and had been a crew member since 1994. In the back of my mind, I knew I was ready for another assignment. When we set out to sea from St. Marteen, I was not officially on the watch bill but went to the starboard bridge wing, out of the way, but able to keep an eye on things. It was a straightforward sea detail. We just had to bring in the anchor, turn toward Puerto Rico, and head out by following our navigation track.

Disaster

As we manned up, a mega tourist ship pulled into port and weighed anchor literally a few hundred yards ahead of us. It normally takes us about forty-five minutes from manning up to get underway, with some of the underway checklists supervised and verified by the duty department heads. We had a Collection, Holding, and Transfer (CHT) barge attached to the port side of the ship. Somehow it took her more time than usual to get disconnected, and we spent a few minutes waiting for the engineers to report that line was disconnected, and we were free to maneuver. We turned starboard, passing that big cruise liner on our port side, but the whole time the CHT barge was also heading out to sea and remained on course on our starboard side. Therefore, we did not immediately turn toward our starboard side to intercept the course to our next destination. Therefore, we were a bit left off track.

The young man at Wadi Rum finds serenity in the desert.
— Chapter 13, p. 198

With Admiral Mike Mullen, 17th Chairman of the Joint Chiefs of Staff.
He was visiting us in Kuwait.
— Chapter 11, p. 177

Dr. Javier Stuppard and his trombone at my military retirement ceremony.
– Chapter 13, p. 200

I was in the Pentagon on 9/11, and now "Here I am, in Baghdad!"
– Chapter 13, p. 175

The NATO SNMG2 warships' commanding officers and senior leaders.
– Chapter 10, p. 157

With General Stéphane Abrial (French Air Force), Commander Allied Transformation Command (2009–2012), the first European to be appointed permanently as head of a NATO strategic command, and Admiral Rob Bauer (Royal Netherlands Navy), the 33rd Chair of the Military Committee of the North Atlantic Treaty Organization (NATO, 2021–2025) at the 2024 ACT change of command in Norfolk, VA. – Chapter 13, p. 208

My three sons during our tour in Hawaii.
– Chapter 5, p. 72

My Father Maurice in his
late 20's.
– Chapter 1, p. 2

My Mother Gracieuse in her
late 20's.
– Chapter 1, p. 2

My three sons Javier, Valentino, and Charles and my wife Nidda.
– Chapter 13, p. 208

My wife Nidda, the rock of my life.
– Chapter 14, p. 210

With my two favorite ladies, my mother Grace and my wife Nidda after
my retirement at the Naval War College in Newport, RI.
– Chapter 13, p. 200

Four brothers on vacation trying to solve the world's problems.
– Chapter 13, p. 208

Then another cruise ship tracked right toward us for a starboard passage, or what we call in nautical terminology, a closest point of approach (CPA) on the starboard side. As the cruise liner got closer to CPA, XO was on the starboard bridge wing with me; we were both present but stayed out of the way of the bridge team. As we watched the two ships passing each other in the morning, we kept heading away from our laid-out track, which was to our starboard side. Once we passed the cruise liner, again it would be a matter of coming right to intercept our track and head toward our destination.

That's when I heard a vibration noise below deck. It was not the consistent noise I was used to hearing, being on that part of the ship. I told the XO that I believed that noise was coming from the radar room right below us on the starboard bridge wing. He told me he thought it was from a morpack valve further down in the passageway. I decided to go down to the radar room to satisfy my curiosity. I had just made it to the bottom of the ladder when I felt the ship shake. Damn it, I thought to myself, I should have come down faster. It could be that one of my pumps or something else just blew up. I rushed toward the equipment room, then I felt another ship vibration coming from the aft part of the ship on the starboard side.

Reassured that the sound wasn't originating from my combat system spaces, I ran upstairs to the bridge. When I got back to the bridge, I heard the captain giving the following command: "This is the captain, I have the deck and the conn." Conning a ship is the act of steering or controlling a ship. I knew immediately that something was very wrong. I went to the quartermaster's chart table and in a low voice asked, "What just happened?"

He told me he thought that we had hit something. I looked at the chart and saw the track. According to the chart on the bridge, we were passing close to an underway water sea mount, but we were not heading directly for it. The CPA, though, would be close to the starboard side.

I then immediately went down to the CIC. The navigation chart showed we were heading directly to the sea mount. I asked the chief what happened? According to that chart, we had been tracking toward the underwater obstacle for some time to avoid the cruise liner. The chief told me that he has been reporting it to the bridge via the phone talker. I immediately went back up to the bridge and asked the phone talker if he had been reporting the danger to the bridge. He said that he had but in the final moment was told by the navigator to "shut up," maybe not using these exact two words, but the phone talker stopped making his report and the bridge team was trying to figure out what was going on. (We learned later that a hurricane the year before had moved the buoy marking the danger.)

The ship was at all stop. The damage control central went down for any damage assessment and there was no apparent flooding in the ship. The captain decided to test our maneuverability. We went ahead one third on the port unaffected engine, and it was okay. Then he ordered stop. Next, he ordered starboard engine ahead one third, and I experienced something that I have never experienced before on a ship – it was as if the ship had a flat tire. It felt like it was wobbling in the water.

The captain immediately ordered us to stop. We decided to lock the starboard shaft and try to make it to Puerto Rico at five miles an hour on the port engine. It took us a few hours and soon we were there. We sent the immediate messages to Navy Headquarters telling our bosses what had just happened. The captain to his credit ordered me to take immediate custody of the charts that were being used on the bridge and in CIC. I took the charts and locked them in my safe in my stateroom, so no one could have access to them except myself.

When we arrived in Puerto Rico that evening, the mood in the ship was quite somber. Later, on land, at an officer get together on the beach, I saw the captain walking by himself near the edge of the water, and I joined him there. I did not look at him and I did not address him, but I thought he needed someone to be there with him. Without looking at me, he said, "Charles, I am thinking about the poem written by Conrad about the burden of command." I had read that poem as well a few years ago in the US Naval Institute's famous *Command at Sea* book. It was a passage from another book and movie, *The Cruel Sea*. It says:

> "… In each ship there is one man who, in the hour of emergency or peril at sea, can turn to no other man. There is one who alone is ultimately responsible for the safe navigation, engineering performance, accurate gunfire or morale of the ship. He is the Commanding Officer. He is the ship! … This is the most difficult and demanding assignment in the Navy. There is not an instant during his tour as Commanding Officer that he can escape the grasp of command responsibility. His privileges, in view of his obligations, are almost ludicrously small; nevertheless, this is the spur which has given the Navy its greatest leaders. It is a duty which richly deserves the highest, time-honored title of the seafaring world – Captain."

He told me that he doubted he would be in command of the ship by tomorrow. He realized that something had gone terribly wrong, and like any good CO, he was ready to take his punishment. Just like the cruel sea, our Navy is unforgiving when it comes to certain mistakes. As officers we all know what we signed up for, our line of work is unforgiving and demands absolute accountability. I had no words of wisdom to offer to him in this gravest moment – just my presence.

Shortly thereafter, the naval investigation into the incident began. The next day, we reported to the designated room at the appointed time, and there were only six officers present. First, the SURFLANT Chief of Staff called in the navigator, then the conning officer. The OOD was called, and I went in with him as a character witness. He was asked a few questions which he answered. The COS never addressed me and did not ask me any questions. Then the CO was called. We all waited outside the room. He was in there for a longer time than the other officers. He came out, and I followed him to his car. He did not look at me and did not say a word. He got in, and I saw a few tears falling off his cheek before he drove away.

Later, LT Phil Sobeck and I – who had worked very closely with the CO in the commissioning of the ship – went to see him at his bachelor officer quarters (BOQ) room. He was more composed and told me that for twenty-plus years he has always been on the opposite side of the podium; this is the first time he was on this side of it. The person on the other side is so powerful it is overwhelming; the person standing in judgment is such an all-powerful presence. More to the point, the COS had made him feel like shit. For over twenty years, he has given his life to our Navy, and with one mistake, he was being treated like a common criminal.

He did not mind accepting his punishment, and he acknowledged his mistake. But what galled him was how the judging officer made him feel. Then the CO left me with these pearls of wisdom. He said, "Charles, you will be a CO someday. When you take a crew member to captain's mast, just remember to let him retain his dignity. You can punish the crew, but you do not have to crush them." These words became engraved in my mind as if etched in stone.

Great leaders are fair leaders. They may judge, but they do not humiliate. People make mistakes, and certain mistakes can't be forgiven. But as they say, to err is human. People in positions of power also need to be human. I vowed to myself that when I became a CO, I would do everything in my power to treat people fairly and empathetically.

Our captain never returned to the ship. Same evening, another captain who was supposed to report to DDG-61 instead was immediately flown into our ship. When he arrived, we briefed him on everything that happened. He said to assemble the crew on the flight deck. It was good that he decided to speak to the crew sooner than later; they all wanted to know the intention of this new CO and of what he was made.

First impressions count, especially after a difficult incident.

The CO began by telling the crew who he was. He said that he personally knew the last CO and that they were friends. He explained how this was a bittersweet moment for him; sweet because he has been waiting all his life to take command of a warship as a Naval Academy graduate; bitter because he personally knew our former captain was a good man and a good officer. This recognition of the old CO as a good man was a generous and kind gesture – it earned our respect.

Taking over from a beloved commander is challenging. Some come in and bad-mouth the previous leader. Others act as if the previous individual never existed. Still others are quick to assert their absolute authority.

The first action of this CO was to participate in our scheduled physical readiness test the next morning, and he ended up running with the fastest guys in the crew, like Who is this? – and finishing first. That impressed everyone. More impressive, though, was that he didn't beat anyone up about the previous incident at sea. He didn't tell us how incompetent we were, and that he was there to whip us into shape. And he continued to speak compassionately about our former captain.

He modeled how to assume command in the wake of a crisis. By being kind, by never blaming, by demonstrating his willingness to be part of the crew, he earned our loyalty.

Maintaining Self-respect

A towing ship, USNS Hugo was ordered from Norfolk to tow us all the way from Puerto Rico to Norfolk. As the senior watch officer, I recommended to the CO and XO that we maintain the regular watch rotation, with all watch stations manned. We were an American Warship and there was no way we were going to use the excuse of not being able to go under our own power to shirk our responsibilities. After all, we had electricity and our combat system was working. We stood the watch, even the officer of the deck watch and the conning officer watch and every other required watch. We stayed alert and conducted training during the long transit, but it was a humbling experience – we were being towed by a ship much smaller and less powerful than our own.

After the 1997 New Year celebrations, we arrived at the Portland Naval shipyard and went straight to the block. Once the water was drained, we all finally got a chance to see the damage. The sonar dome was damaged, but there was no puncture. Three propeller blades were missing, and they were all recovered by Navy divers. One of our reduction gear transmissions was shut and had to be replaced, and we had to use the Navy's battle spare. As the repairs Commenced, the captain never moved his office off the ship, despite the noise and the dust. He told me that having his office on the ship will force the officers and the crew to come more often to the ship (from the barge where they were temporarily being housed). He did not want to totally abandon USS Gonzalez to the yard workers; he wanted to maintain ownership of the ship.

Captains don't abandon ships. Symbolic actions are important to leaders. Many times, they communicate more than words ever can.

The mighty warship USS Gonzalez finally got repaired and we returned to the fleet better than new. We were ready to start the training cycle for a newly commissioned US ship and were eager to start; we just needed a chance to prove it to the rest of the Navy and the world. As CSO, I had nine officers and a crew of over 100 technicians under my direct leadership. I was also the Combat System Team Trainer (CSTT) and acted as the Integrated Training Team (ITT) Leader. As ITT, I oversaw integrating the various shipboard team trainers.

The time came for me to leave the ship – I was looking forward to a new challenge. Prior to my departure, the CO requested that I stay until we passed our final battle problem. He said, "Charles, I know you have been here onboard for a long time, but I would like you to stay mainly in charge of the ITT to get the ship through the training phase." I gladly accepted. We went through the training phase and passed with flying colors.

After three years onboard this "fine naval vessel" (as Star Trek's Scotty referred to the Starship Enterprise), it was time to move on. I received orders to travel to Newport and study at the Naval War College. I left the USS Gonzalez in July 1997. The CO asked me to write a Plan Of the Day (POD) note to the crew to announce my departure. I wrote it and showed it to him, he made some minor edits and I gave it to the XO for the POD. Here it is:

4. **FROM LCDR STUPPARD:** I reported aboard GONZALEZ 10 October 1994 as Combat Systems Officer (CSO). I have seen the ship go through Construction, Light-Off, Testing and Trials and have had the pleasure to welcome most of you as Senior Watch Officer. My tour on board as CSO was absolutely the best out of four ships. As of 0700, Today, I will formally turn over "CSO" to my relief, LT Vandroff. I have received orders to go to the Naval War College in Newport, RI and slated to be the second XO of a DDG currently being built in Bath. I will also be relieved as Senior Watch Officer by LCDR Panoff at 0800, 1 October 1997. I will continue working on Integrated Team Training (ITT) and Combat System Training Team (CSTT) in preparation for CART on 20-24 October and will detach on 24 October 1997. I thank you all for your support. *USS Gonzalez POD note, per CO request*

Chapter 7

On the Path to Becoming a Commander

I was always fascinated by the Naval War College. Even when I went to Newport and to some other Navy schools, I would manage to drive around the war college buildings or go to the museum. Once I even went inside and ended up in the war college library. I picked up a book and sat in one of the cubicles overlooking the mighty Newport bridge. Never did I think that I would one day be a student at the Naval War College. Back as a division officer when I first joined the Navy, I picked up a copy of the history of the Naval War College, and I read it during my first deployment on Med 3–88 on the USS Biddle.

Right after I was selected for XO by the Navy selection board, I called my detailer, and he assigned me to be the second XO of a brand-new destroyer still being built in Bath; I contacted the ship and started tracing her progress. I even met the next CO of the ship, CDR Pete Gumataotao, and I started to build that relationship. I then asked my detailer to assign me to the Naval War College for a quick year before I reported as second XO of USS Decatur (DDG 73).

A Return to a Different Type of College

I reported to Newport in August after taking some time off. To be assigned to the Naval War College for me was even beyond a dream come true – I never thought that I was good enough to attend such a prestigious school.

I went to the store and got myself two new suits and a few ties because I would not be wearing a uniform to class. I felt like a kindergarten boy heading out to school for the very first time. I was up by 0400, although I did not have to report until 0800, and class was only a short five minutes away. The first day of class, all students reported to the auditorium for an introductory session where we were told about our seminar. The entire class was divided into small seminars.

The Naval War College consisted of three trimesters: Joint Military Operation (JMO), National Security and Decision Making (NSDM), and Strategy and Policy (S&P). I would start with JMO. We only had about fifteen students in our seminar, and it was fully joint with folks from the Army, Air Force, Marine Corps, and other US Agencies such as Federal Bureau of Investigation (FBI), National Security Agency (NSA), and Department of State (DOS). This mix of talent and perspective is by design, providing a broad perspective to our nation's future leaders.

We had two instructors assigned to us, a US Navy SH-60 aviator captain, and a US Marine Corps colonel. Each seminar had two assigned professors. Naval War College was like drinking from a fire hydrant, and I opened my mind wide.

Leaders learn. They acquire knowledge with the avarice of miners panning for gold. Knowledge provides an edge in decision-making, and it offers wisdom to deal with challenging situations. Leadership learning shouldn't be confined to one's specific area of expertise. The broader your knowledge, the better your leadership perspective.

At the college, each student had to take two electives. Mine were "War and Religion" and "Intelligence for the Commander."

We would study a religion a week under our teacher who was a Navy chaplain. He would bring an expert on that specific religion for each session. We had a course on Judaism, and he brought a rabbi to talk to us – I'd never met a rabbi before. He offered his perspective about the Bible, Judaism, and mostly Jerusalem, and how important and crucial that city is for the Jewish people. The following week, our chaplain had us meet Iman Habibi, a practitioner of Islam. He spoke about Islam, and I placed myself in his shoes and attempted to see what he saw – he told us about the great city of Jerusalem and how important and crucial that city is for Muslims throughout the world. The following week, we had a Christian pastor full of energy who presented the Christian perspective. Though this was a perspective with which I was familiar, I had never viewed it in relation to the two other religions.

I came to understand that the issues facing us as a human race are complex and difficult, especially in view of the passions people attach to most of them; that these passions are not always directed by reason and intellectual analysis; that these passionate beliefs can spiral out of control, and they end up on the battlefield.

All this helped me grasp that my job wasn't only to be a Navy ship driver but to also be a citizen-soldier, a type of military/ statesman.

I took courses in a variety of subjects, from resource allocation to the Force Planning process. During the second term, I learned I'd been reslated and as a result missed the chance to serve with my good friend CDR Pete Gumataotao.

During my last semester, I took a seminar on Strategy and Policy (S&P) given by one of the best instructors, Dr. Alberto Coll. In S&P, we did one war a week (except for the American Revolution and the Civil War which took two weeks). We started with Thucydides' Peloponnesian War, then the French Revolution and Vietnam all the way to the Gulf War. One day, my seminar got an assignment to read an eight-page paper, then to come to class and discuss it. I did the reading and underlined the appropriate sections in which I was interested. When class convened though, I discovered that my classmates all had different perspectives on the topic based on their own backgrounds and service. Then I realized why nations fight. The very same information is viewed and interpreted from people's own perspective.

Whether you're a general or a CEO or the head of a bank or a hospital, you're going to receive wildly different opinions from your people. Instead of becoming upset or taking sides, you need to weigh the differing perspectives and come up with a frame that makes sense to you.

Finally, it was time to graduate. The College helped me realize that a world of non-engineering existed. I was always into Math and Science where 1+1=2. At the war college, I learned that sometimes what you see may not be what is.

As a leader, you must be aware that things are not always the way they seem, especially in the world of diplomacy and international relations.

After graduating, I called the Armed Forces Staff College in Norfolk for the phase II completion of my joint professional military education (JPME) and managed to attend for 10 weeks before heading to Bermuda to meet my reassigned ship on its way back from deployment. They swung by and picked me up, and I boarded the USS Nicholas (FFG 47) and started my turnover as XO.

USS Nicholas 1999–2000

The Navy taught me the value of adapting to new situations. Things change, and we must always adapt to new situations. I switched my mindset, helping myself adapt to the new job of being an XO.

Earlier, I had taken a course at Surface Warfare School Command (SWOS), and the case study of USS Gonzalea came up—a case that illustrates the potential problems in the CO-XO relationship. The instructor didn't know that I was onboard the ship. He started talking about the case based on his reading of the official investigation. He said "the sour relationship between the CO and the XO" created serious problems that led to the ship striking another ship. The instructor explained that the CO would not listen to the XO's recommendations.

I raised my hand, described how I was on the Gonzalez, and was given permission to explain what really took place. Case studies are designed to identify the reason bad things happen–the relationship between what we call string of events, like if this one thing did not happen, then it would have prevented that other thing from happening. A basic flaw exists in this analytical method– it tends to be revisionist. In hindsight, as we look at various events that affect the timeline of an accident, we can always draw a linear line between the events and make them fit a certain post-event pattern. This is where the analysis becomes flawed. We force specific events to fit the curve, but it's all framed in hindsight. We know the result we are looking for, the end of the story. Have you ever attempted to analyze an event that was prevented by someone not doing a certain thing? This is a type of negative proof, and it's very difficult to say if Mary failed to do Y or John X, then Z wouldn't have happened.

I explained to the class that the CO did not have a bad relationship with the XO before the incident. And that this fictional bad relationship had nothing to do with the actual accident. CO and XO occasionally have bad relationships, but these relationships don't produce ship collisions or groundings.

The value of a case study is that it can teach us to avoid mistakes or employ useful behaviors when we encounter similar situations. The problem, though, is that there's no guarantee that if we change our thinking or actions based on the case study that we'll change the outcome of a situation.

Over the years, I've learned the most from situations in which I was personally involved. Based on this situation, I learned a lesson that helped me as an XO. I was always on the bridge with the CO, and I was always a forceful back up for him. There was no way on my watch I would let the ship get into danger without being fully engaged (I certainly didn't want to be the object of a case study).

All leaders are exposed to case histories, and they can be good sources of learning. But they should also be taken with a grain of salt, since unless you're there with boots on the ground, you may receive the wrong message from just reading about it.

I began my XO experience when the NICHOLAS picked me up in Bermuda. Upon arriving to homeport at the Norfolk Naval Shipyard, the CO went on leave, and I immediately went from XO to becoming the acting CO of the ship (when the CO is on leave for more than four days, the XO becomes acting CO).

I saw my XO tour as a perfect laboratory to learn how to be a CO. I was second in command, and I had someone to ask questions about command. In a way, it was a perfect apprenticeship for a leader. My tour was tough at times but, I did not see it as such – it was a tremendous learning environment. This was my last step to obtain my command qualification board. There was nothing to really study for the board, members would include current commanding officers of our squadron.

I recognized that they would ask me about my command philosophy. Therefore, I started jotting notes down and thinking about this topic. I read about the command philosophy of others and considered my own in this context. Then I scheduled the board with the commodore and the CO's.

When I went before them, sure enough skipper Joe Murphy wanted to know about my command philosophy. I said one tenet of my philosophy is to make command fun and ensure my crew has a fun time onboard. He responded, "What is fun about mid-watches? What is fun about a young seaman swabbing the deck?"

I tried to explain but probably wasn't very convincing expressing my ideas. Nonetheless, I passed the board and obtained a favorable recommendation, and the Commodore certified me as "command worthy." That was a big step in my life. I had the blessings of several American ship Captains as being worthy of command myself; it was a day of which to be proud. I sent that paper to the board and now all I had to do was to wait for the result of the board. I went back to doing my job as an XO.

Later, the annual CDR Command board met in Millington, TN. The notification of CO's selection is done by a flag officer, and I got a telephone call at home from one of my favorite flag officers, RADM Dan Holloway. He said congratulations, I was selected as a CO. It was such a beautiful feeling! The next Monday, I went to work, and I learned that out of over twelve hundred naval officers eligible for command at sea, the Navy only picked 73, and I was one of them as well as the current Vice Joint Chief of Staff, Admiral Chris Grady. But I also prayed for those who did not get selected and asked God to give them strength, for I knew how disappointed they must have been.

Achieving leadership milestones like this one is useful. They boost self-confidence and provide proof that you're worthy of whatever promotion you receive. Just about everyone has a nagging voice in his or her head suggesting that he or she isn't worthy. This type of milestone counteracts this voice, and if it doesn't completely erase self-doubt, it minimizes its negative effects.

Prevention is Worth a Pound of Cure

Whenever we were underway, I would always be on the bridge on the opposite side of the CO's location, looking at what he was not looking. For the navigator's report, I had the port lookout watches trained to report to me what buoy number we were passing. They would say, "XO, passing buoy number 5," and I would acknowledge them. I told them to require an acknowledgment from me—if I did not give them some type of acknowledgement then, I did not get it. As a result, when navigating a channel, I always knew where we were.

I always had the navigation chart open in front of my chair, and I would mark the buoys we just passed; I would always be aware of the ship's location in the channel. One day, we were going inside the channel into Norfolk and somehow, the CO was distracted by a report; bad events always start like that, a minor distraction causes people to lose focus on the most immediate concern. I knew we were supposed to turn before the next set of buoys. After receiving the report, we had passed buoy number X; but the ship kept approaching the buoys as if to take it on the wrong side. I asked the OOD what he was doing, and he said he would turn after this buoy in front of us. I asked the navigator to verify and he hesitated, since he was just repeating the recommendation of his team to the OOD. When he looked up at the window, he did not really know which buoy was which. The CO, for one second, also didn't know where we were.

I ordered the OOD to turn immediately: "Turn left standard rudder now!" The CO was surprised by my command, but I showed him where we were on the map and what buoy we were looking at, and he soon concurred. My awareness of our current position probably saved the ship.

If you relied on case studies to teach you how to deal with this situation, however, you probably wouldn't have dealt with it successfully. Case studies focus on learning from mistakes with negative consequences, but here, there were no negative consequences. I would guess that several such occasions are prevented every day by our mariners at sea. In fact, 99% of collisions and groundings are prevented daily in the performance of our duty. But the ones that get reported and make big news are the ones that someone could not prevent.

This has two concerning outcomes. First, it creates negative publicity for the Navy and for Captains – people wonder who in the world is running the ship? And second, few people are aware of all the insight and expertise that continuously prevent accidents at sea. What we do is inherently dangerous. By anticipating these dangers and training ourselves to avoid them, we create the illusion that it's not very dangerous at all.

Sometimes, leadership is a thankless job. People are thanked for solving problems but not for preventing them. Still, I derived satisfaction from preventative tactics, as I think many leaders derive satisfaction from avoiding obstacles and traps that can sink their organizations.

Management by Walking Around...the Deck

I continued to learn onboard NICHOLAS, and I continued to polish my command philosophy, the one I had written for my command qualification board. During my XO tour, we were no longer requiring Planned Maintenance spot checks, the rationale being that it was a waste of manpower and leadership time. As XO, there are certain things that I did like a religion–spot checking and berthing inspections being two of them. They allowed me to take a break from the daily and excruciating administrative work of the XO behind a desk. I had the opportunity to interface with the crew. At 1000, every day, I asked the Master at Arms to come to my office and pick me up. It didn't matter what else I was doing; I'd drop it since this was sacred time between me, my MAA, and the berthing cleaners. We had a ritual from which we did not deviate, and the crew and I enjoyed it. I would go to the berthing; the one cleaner would call himself to attention on deck and present his space, and I would say "very well," and we would go on inspecting. The crew would inspect with me. First, I asked the cleaner if he was ready and if he thinks I could find anything wrong with his berthing. Some said "no," some hesitated, but in either case, we would go on inspecting the berthing. Part of my objective was teaching them how to inspect a berthing which I had learned from an INSURV inspector before becoming an XO. I had asked the professionals how to do a proper berthing inspection, and one inspector took the time to show me. I enjoyed finding dirty spots that the crew missed, and I could tell they were thinking, "How does the XO know to look into this or that corner?" All this work paid off; in that we received excellent rating when we had an inspection while I was XO. And that was the second benefit: The crew took pride in the rating achieved because they had all worked hard and intelligently to achieve it.

I continued to do spot checks after everyone else had stopped doing them, and the CO asked why. I told him it was my chance to see the crew and the equipment. Once a week I would pick one random division and conduct a maintenance check, from engineering to ops to supply to combat system. Later, SURFLANT would realize that it was a mistake not to conduct spot checks since equipment on ships started to fail or did not perform as per specifications. My motivation, though was to get out of my office and keep in touch with the crew.

Leaders can't lead effectively in isolation. They need boots on the ground, and they need to see and talk to their people. That's the only way they can know what's really going on.

Commander

The CDR promotion board result arrived, and I was promoted to O-5, Commander. I exchanged my gold oak leaf for a silver one. I made sure that I called my mentor, Dominick Capuano, who then still lived in Massapequa, Long Island. I said, "Dominick, you're not going to believe this, but I just got promoted to Commander." When I joined the Navy, I did not then know the difference between a LT or a LCDR or a CDR. As far as I was concerned, I joined the Navy to serve and see the world. Making rank was not part of it, yet I was making rank.

I called my detailer and started discussing possibilities for the next job. I told him I want to go to the Joint Staff, which I liked when I was at the War College. During the final exercise problem for Joint Military Operations, I took on the role of chairman of the Joint Chiefs of Staff, the person in charge of the entire US military machine, reporting to the Secretary of Defense and to the President of the United States. The detailer told me I could go wherever I wanted and proposed three jobs where there were openings: J-8 Budget, J-5 Strategy and Plans, or J-3 Operations. I chose the J-5 job because I liked the "big-think" piece of it. The detailer said he would propose me and send my name up to the Joint staff. Two days later, the CO got a phone call from the Joint Staff, and he gave me a thumbs up. The Captain asked that I come up to the Pentagon for an interview the next day. I drove there and reported to J-5. I was interviewed by a Navy captain who already had my records from the Bureau of Naval personnel, so I guessed he wanted to see me in person. Then I went to interview with his boss, the Division Chief and Air Force officer by the name of Colonel Fadock. I made a good impression on him, apparently, since a few days later, I got an email from the Joint Staff Navy Captain, and he said I was selected for the job. I contacted my detailer, and he said I am good to go and would receive orders soon. I was on cloud 9! This would be my first real shore duty since joining the Navy, because at the War College, I was a student and did not actually have to do any staff work.

I prepared to leave my post as XO. I had one final trip onboard and then, would be relieved by another officer. When the time came to turn everything over to this officer, I made an effort to supply him with everything he needed and was respectful and generous with my time. He asked me why I was treating him so nicely. I suppose it was because of the way I was "raised" – what I had been taught by other officers when I was starting out in the Navy. And I suppose part of it was my upbringing.

Leaders who treat others with respect can expect respect in return.

I departed the ship and checked into a hotel for the night. I received my plaque from the CO, but it was missing the front glass – no one had bothered to check if it was there prior to our departure. I accepted it but as a reminder, I left it without a glass cover and never bought one for it. It is still one of my only plaques that's missing the glass covering. It reminds me what happens when there's a lack of attention to details.

I boarded the train from Maine to Boston's Logan airport and flew back to Virginia Beach. I took a few days off and got ready mentally to start my first assignment in Washington, D.C., the Pentagon. It was September 2000.

Chapter 8

In the Heart of the Pentagon

*A*s I've noted earlier, leaders prepare. They prepare for big things, and they prepare for small ones. On a ship, knowing where everything is can be a matter of life and death. But it can also be important on land.

The Pentagon is a big place where one can easily get lost. To prepare myself for this assignment, I read *Assignment Pentagon*, a book written by Major General Perry M. Smith and Colonel Daniel M. Gerstein. It was well worth it. The Pentagon is like 25 five-story buildings packed into one structure. Looking from the Washington monument or the Mall side, one sees the first five-story building, between corridor 9 and 10, which is where I worked. But one sees only the outer building or the E-ring. Four other inner rings (D–A) contain additional buildings, and locating yourself and finding a particular office can be daunting without a good map. My reference book had all the trivia and the office numbering system in it. I made sure I studied that book thoroughly before reporting to my duty station.

My office was in 2D948; I had been there before for my interview, so I knew exactly how to find it. I reported to work on day 1, eager and excited to start this new adventure.

To enter my place of work, I had to go through several security stations. The physical location of our workplace was a secure area since we focused on United States political and military policy and strategy. My new division was a joint organization. We had folks from the Air Force, Army, Navy, Marine Corps, and several others on a temporary one-year assignment from NSA, State Department, NIMA, etc.

I was working with highly accomplished leaders from different military branches. The J-5 Deputy Director for Pol-Mil Affairs Europe was then a two-star Army officer, MG Keith Dayton, who would retire as a three star later. He led three divisions. The second division was the Russian division, and they dealt primarily with US/Russian military policy; Division Chief was Air Force Colonel Boudreaux. The third division consisted Country Engagement officers and policy officers under Colonel Church. My branch, the first division, was the policy section, and our interaction was primarily with NATO at the Military Committee level. We had a US organization under a three-star assigned to Brussels and he led the US team that interfaced constantly with NATO; we were their US counterparts. I had a Navy Captain in that organization who was my direct counterpart – Captain Dowling, a helicopter pilot. My job was to be his Joint Staff link and provide him with whatever US policy and perspective he needed to do his job.

Our boss in NATO Policy was Colonel Jean-Marc "Juice" Jouas, a superbly nice F-16 Fighter pilot who would rise to be a three-star leading the US Forces in Korea. He was assisted by the able Mr. Stu Drury a super smart West Point graduate who spent his early years in the US Army, he had a master's from Harvard. My branch chief was Colonel Pete Dillon, one of the nicest bosses I have ever had. He would later go on to take command of a Special Forces Group (SFG) at Fort Bragg.

Leaders learn from other leaders, and I had more knowledge and expertise in my group than seemed possible.

High-Level, Multifaceted Responsibilities

The ability to handle a range of complex tasks in volatile environments is crucial to effective leadership, whether in the military, business or government.

At the Pentagon, I learned this skill. My portfolio consisted of NATO Force Structure, NATO Command Structure, and NATO Training Exercise and Equipping, dealing primarily with nations aspiring to become NATO members.

NATO Force Structure was my busiest portfolio as I worked with my counterpart in Belgium on US political-military policy involving NATO. As the political landscape was changing, the primary US concern was the relevancy of NATO. It had to be a robust and credible force. NATO at first only worked in its backyard, but as focus and threats shifted away from Europe, we had to continue to engage the world. NATO needed to be able to operate and participate elsewhere, but their force structure was not built and created for that. Their primary focus used to be the big bear next door. The goal, then, was to create forces that were able to deploy out of area. Creating the NATO High Readiness Forces Headquarters was the first step.

My next portfolio was NATO Command Structure. Since World War II, NATO has been led by two US General Officers. One in SHAPE (Supreme Headquarters Allied Powers Europe) Belgium and the other in Norfolk, VA. Our effort was to reorganize NATO to keep it relevant. We started working toward changing the headquarters in Norfolk. First was a name change and a mission change.

During this time, I served as the Action Officer for our chairman (CJCS)'s participation in the upcoming NATO Military Committee/Chief of Defense (CHOD) Session (MCCS) and had to go to Belgium as a member of the official US delegation.

Preparing the Chairman's briefing book was a major feat that required various point papers from several other action officers. One such action officer was an Army Major Chris Cavoli who worked the Russian desk – (as of today 2024, Chris is General Chris Cavoli, serving as Supreme Headquarters Allied Commander, Europe). I attended the meeting where all of NATO's top commanders were present. The room had a large circular sitting area, and all the NATO country representatives were there. The head of the Russian military was also present.

Seated next to CJCS was the UK CHOD, and from whom earlier in the year we had been invited to hear a brief, followed by a Q&A. The session was very frank, and it was a unique opportunity for a young officer to hear and speak to such a senior level officer. I sat across from the Russian chief of defense, and he kept looking at me quizzically. I tried to imagine what could be going inside the mind of the Russian chief of defense and what kind of questions or concern he had as he looked at me. Perhaps he was intrigued because I was the only Black person there (though I was not the first Black person to be in that room, since General Colin Powell had attended plenty of MCCS). The meeting adjourned, and we drove back to the C–17 airplane waiting to take us back to Washington, D.C.

The experience was unforgettable. I had been with the top commanders of the most powerful nations on earth discussing the most intricate defense issues of the time.

We all grow from experiences that involve new responsibilities and high-level performers – handling these experiences competently give us confidence. Being part of an elite leadership group and having conversations that were insightful and important helped me feel like I belonged.

Back in the Pentagon, I continued to work my main portfolio consisting of NATO High Readiness Force Headquarters (HRF/HQ). I organized several meetings and had to do a significant amount of travel – Milan, Valencia, Istanbul. I was becoming more worldly in the best sense of that term.

Much more so today than in the past, leaders need to possess a global consciousness – an ability to work with people from various backgrounds and cultures. Through my NATO work, I was gaining this global exposure.

Back in the Pentagon, I started working the final brief to get permission for US military personnel to participate as members of the various NATO High Readiness Forces Headquarters from Secretary Donald Rumsfeld. I prepared my boss Colonel Pete Dillon for a tank session with the Chairman and the Joint Staff. He gave them the brief, and they gave him the go ahead to brief Mr. Rumsfeld – a positive sign. The Secretary finally had the brief and decided to go with "close to" the number of military personnel we had recommended. I wrote "close to" because we recommended no more than 20 and the Secretary decided on 19, as if to make a statement to the Military. No one argued with him. I was just happy he agreed with us and did not kill our recommendation. He had the power to say that he did not want the US to participate in the HRF; though, we would have given him a pushback to show how crucial our participation is for the success of the endeavor. In my studies later of the character of Donald Rumsfeld, I now see his rationale – it was a way of assuming his control of the US military machine; he probably wanted to demonstrate that he was in control.

One day out of the blue, Colonel Jouas asked me to get a NATO High Readiness Forces brief ready for the Deputy Director, Major General Keith Dayton. I worked on it very quickly because by then, I was the Joint Staff expert on all things HRF, since I had spent hours and days thinking about the topic and reading all the NATO documents and providing US input and perspective. I was told that the brief would not be delivered in his office but instead in our NATO conference room. I walked in ready to brief him and was surprised to see the entire division there along with the general. Why would the entire division come to listen to my brief? I wasn't sure, but this wasn't the time or place to ask questions. The General summoned me front and center, and they called "attention to award" and read the citation. Colonel Jouas and the general gave me a Joint Staff Achievement award. If I was surprised when I entered the room, now I was floored.

When I got over my shock, I was enormously grateful for this gesture of appreciation. for all the work I had devoted to the HRF issue. I had worked long hours – I was often in my office after everyone else had gone home, working on the US response to some type of decision NATO needed from all its members. The next morning, I would focus my efforts on obtaining the blessing of proper levels of authority – a variety of director-level people.

Everyone needs validation. Leaders gain confidence as they gain authority if people they respect approve of their efforts. It doesn't matter if that approval comes in the form of a formal gesture, such as my award or if it is merely a verbal "job well done." While many leaders project an air of self-confidence, there is always some doubt behind what the world sees. Obtaining pats on the back regularly helps keep that doubt from interfering with one's work.

Life in the Joint Staff was never boring; there was always plenty of action to keep an action officer occupied. I was applying for jobs there that would offer me greater responsibility and challenges, and though I didn't get the first three for which I applied – Executive Assistant to DJS, VCJCS, and CJCS – I kept trying.

If you aspire to significant leadership positions, you must accept that you're going to have to try and fail more than once before you're selected.

Part of my portfolio was NATO training and evaluation; therefore, I was assigned to be the Crisis Management Exercise Officer for my J-5 Deputy Directorate. We had to run an exercise once, and it was quite a learning experience for me, since we had to brief very high-ranking officers. *Becoming comfortable and confident dealing with high-level leaders is part of a process that everyone who aspires to be one of those leaders needs to go through.* I also applied for and was accepted to work at Site R – this was the name for the Raven Rock Mountain complex, a communications and relocation underground facility run by the Pentagon (as described on the internet). The first time I went there – a bus ride that took a few hours – I was surprised that the only signage indicating this was a government facility was a sign that read "Restricted area, US Government property." I stayed there overnight as part of the exercise team. While I can't talk about my day of training there, I can say that it would be useful on 9/11.

Another Day That Will Live in Infamy

September 10, 2001 was a day like any other day. I went to work, did what I had to do, went back home to get ready for another day in the Pentagon. No one could have imagined what the next day would bring. I was on the phone with Captain Dowling and we were discussing some issues about his most recent meeting. Captain Dowling was in Belgium and I was in the Pentagon. Then he told me to wait in a shocked voice, and in the silence that followed I sensed something was terribly wrong. He came back on the line and said that CNN was on and he had just seen a plane hitting the World Trade Center. He said he would call me later. I left my desk and headed toward the TV to turn it on. On my way, I told Colonel Jouas to come with me, something just happened, and it was not good. I turned the TV on CNN and there it was. We saw the tape of the first airplane hitting the World Trade Center.

Colonel Jean-Marc Jouas is an F-16 fighter pilot, as he watched it, he said "This is no accident! The airplane profile shows definite intent." As we watched CNN, we saw the words scrolling at the bottom of the screen reporting a fire in the Pentagon. The other Action Officers who were working on hot projects were not watching TV with us; they kept on working unaware of the events. I knew what had to be done. I walked through the SCIF room telling people to shut down their computers, telling them of the report of a fire in the Pentagon. I went to the front door of our office in 2D948. The letters and numbers signified that we were on the second floor, in the D ring which is a ring right before the famous E ring that faces outside (the A-ring is the inner ring and faces inside the pentagon, and in the ninth corridor by the metro station and the main cafeteria, in room number 48). I peeked outside the room to the right from the D-ring toward the ninth corridor. I saw a long line of people exiting to the right toward the E-Ring. I then told our folks that people were evacuating the building. A bit later, the alarm started to sound. We turned our computers off, secured the materials we were working on and headed outside. I was the mustering officer for our division. I had the list of all personnel next to my desk, and as I had been trained to do, grabbed it and headed outside. The crowd of people exiting was very disciplined. There was no screaming and no running. Everyone acted professionally.

On my way outside, I was wondering how anyone could bring any type of explosive inside the Pentagon given the tight security. It wasn't until we were outdoors, walking around, that I could see the other side of the building and the billowing smoke. In that moment, I understood that we were the perfect target for a terrorist group. Most of the American Joint Staff had gathered in a clump in front of the Pentagon's E-Ring. Others realized that we were sitting ducks, and we were told to spread out and move away from the front of the building.

We followed our training and went to our Fire Drill emergency muster station. I pulled out my list of NATO Division personnel and called people's names – we were all accounted for. Then Colonel Jouas told us to go home and away from the Pentagon. I had taken the metro to come to work that day, and the metro station's entrance was by the A-ring under the tenth corridor. No one was allowed back inside the Pentagon. We were not sure if the building was safe. A fellow Army officer named Tom told me that he drove and would give me a ride to the metro station. On my way, I called my wife on my cell phone. I couldn't reach her. I knew how upset she would be when she heard the news, and so after much effort, I managed to get someone in her office to relay the message that I was okay.

As I walked with Tom toward his car, we heard a loud explosion. I thought it was another bomb. Our reaction was to hurry back home. We knew that we were key members of the Joint Staff and we had to disperse and get away from the area. We could not afford to have all of us killed. The only thought in my mind was the next step. I was a member of a strategic crisis emergency response team. I had to head back home, pack my bag and get to my emergency response station. The original plan had us leaving from the Pentagon in waves, but I could not go back to the Pentagon. So, I packed my bag, got ready and waited a bit before taking action. I tried calling my wife once more but every cell phone system was maxed out and there was no way to get through. I boarded the train, and it was clear that the passengers too were oblivious to the events taking place at the Pentagon. They were on their way from work and hadn't watched the news. The train approached the Pentagon station but did not stop. That was unusual but no one seemed bothered by this odd event.

Unbeknownst to me at the time, the message that I had asked my wife's colleague to relay didn't reach my other family members. My brother Franz who also works in DC called the house in Virginia Beach to inquire whether they know about my whereabouts. He happened to talk to my oldest son, Javier, who had just returned from school. He did not knew what his uncle was talking about, who then told him to turn on the TV. Javier started worrying about me as he watched CNN. It appeared to him that anyone leaving the Pentagon in a stretcher somehow had a resemblance to his dad, and he was by himself in the house. Fortunately, Nidda called home and told him that I was okay.

I received a call from Colonel Jouas in which he said, "Do not head out, come back to work tomorrow, same time!" I was relieved. It meant that what happened at the Pentagon was not "the big one" and the world was still safe. Next morning, I arrived at the Pentagon at my normal time. I reported to the office and turned on the computer and started the day. The rest of the folks started trickling in as well. We heard that President Bush would be

coming to see the chairman and the service chiefs. We began forming teams to put together our response to the attack. In the joint
staff, we had people working with us from various other government departments. In our European division we had people from
National Security Agency [NSA], State Department, and National
Imagery Mapping Agency [NIMA]. During a break in the morning, I ventured out to the main corridor, headed toward the third
deck and toward the sixth corridor where the terrorists' airplane
had hit. I made it all the way inside where I saw broken windows
and burned rooms. The inside of the area was not guarded or taped
yet. I quickly returned to my work area, thinking to myself that
"curiosity kills the cat!"

From this point, we never stopped working. The country was
counting on us. We started getting working responses from our
allies. NATO was ready to invoke Article 5 for us: "if a NATO Ally
is the victim of an armed attack, each and every other member of
the Alliance will consider this act of violence as an armed attack
against all members and will take the actions it deems necessary to
assist the Ally attacked."

NATO voted to send military aid to the US. We accepted their
AWACS to come over and help us fly over the US to provide air
cover. We started flying over New York City and Washington, D.C.
to show the nation that our military was on duty, and we were
ready to protect the American people. Our Action officers in the
J-5 World started working the international piece of the response
plan. The plan eventually became known as 1003V – pronounced
Plan Ten-O-3-Victor.

Our Assistant Deputy Director, Army Colonel Dick Formica
was promoted to Brigadier General and assigned to lead our
Deputy Directorate. He asked me to be his Executive Assistant, and
I gladly accepted.

*Leaders aren't always on the battleground but can contribute as leaders in
other ways. I was used to being a senior officer on a ship – someone who is
potentially in the middle of the action. At the Pentagon, I was working
behind the scenes, but I was learning a lot about research, strategy and*

political-military affairs. In ways, this stretched me as a leader, increasing the breadth and depth of my knowledge. Seeking a diversity of assignments is a great idea for any leader. Not only does it prevent boredom, but it expands your expertise in ways that can be highly useful later in your career.

The Response: Afghanistan, Shock and Awe

The day after 9/11, most of the Joint Staff went to work, and so did many others. We had to find out who committed the terrorist attacks, why the attacks occurred, and then take appropriate actions. As a country, we also had to ensure that never again would we let something like this happen. On the front page of the *New York Times* and several other newspapers, the pictures and the names of the perpetrators were published. The plan that was developed targeted those perpetrators hiding in the mountains of Afghanistan; we were going to obliterate them. Once the plan was firm, reviewed, and blessed by the President of the United States, we went ahead with the execution. We lit up the mountains of Afghanistan and eliminated many of those who were still concocting diabolical plots against the red, white and blue. I will not go into the history of the war in this memoir since there are several books written about it already by leaders and soldiers who were boots on the ground. I am only giving my perspective as a desk officer within the Joint Staff in the Pentagon.

I was grateful to be part of history. Though my role was relatively small, my satisfaction in playing any role in this response to terrorism was huge. Leaders get a chance to make a difference, and all the time I spent in the Pentagon, helping plan a response to 9/11, made me feel like I was part of a team that made a difference.

During the planning phase of the operation, there was a leak in the newspaper. By then, I would say there were less than a thousand people in the Pentagon who knew the details of the plan. As the Executive Assistant of the General Officer in charge of US Strategic Plans and Policy Directorate for the European Theater,

I had access to a lot of information including the CJCS daily intelligence briefs. I was called in by the Office of Special Intelligence for an interview. I bluntly told them I had nothing to do with the press. I also noted that I would never dare compromise our sensitive information because after this job, I intended to be one of the officers who took this fight to the enemy. I was cleared and pressed on with my work. Eventually, the Office of Special Intelligence identified who leaked the information to the press and that person was not military.

A Shift in Targets, Tactics and Jobs

The war in Afghanistan was raging and we were winning. One day, I was watching CNN in the office, and I saw Secretary of State, Colin Powell, testify in front of Congress and declare that Saddam Hussein had weapons of mass destruction (WMD). That testimony changed the course of the war and our efforts in the Pentagon. From that day on, the focus shifted from Afghanistan to Iraq. We had to get those WMDs. All the best minds in our military and civilian counterparts were hard at work to figure out the next step. The war on terror would not just stop in Afghanistan; it would go to wherever it needed, with the end goal of ridding the world of terrorism, once and for all. We were going after the deep roots of this disease.

Leaders pivot. With hindsight, this pivot may not have been exactly in the right direction, given the absence of WMDs. But I witnessed how our leaders shifted their strategy based on the intelligence we were given, the willingness to change thinking and actions based on new information. The takeaway is not that pivoting will always result in positive outcomes, but that this ability is crucial in a volatile world.

The Joint Staff J-5 was a great place to work during this time of crisis. I had a front row seat to the US decision-making apparatus. J-5 has a great working relationship with several other entities and agencies, and I had the opportunity to collaborate with a range of groups. For instance, our Joint Staff people worked with the National Security Council, the Department of State and the War Colleges as well as several think tanks. Again, working with a variety of people with a diversity of expertise was a tremendous experience. Every department and group had its own culture, and I learned how to work with people who had different cultural mindsets than those in Joint Staff or in the Navy. After a while, though, I missed the Navy, and I made known my desire to return to Norfolk.

The Senior Navy Admiral on the Joint Staff asked me where I hoped to go next, and I said anywhere in Norfolk. He told me, "Well, you have the Arleigh Burke." I was flabbergasted!

Leaving the Pentagon was bittersweet. I had learned so much and left as a changed officer with a more strategic view of war. But as the saying goes, the best place to see the Pentagon after working there for a few years is from the rearview mirror – au revoir, Pentagon! Farewell, adieu, and welcome back to the Fleet where I belonged.

Chapter 9

Command of the USS Arleigh Burke (DDG 51)

Preparing for command at sea is a long process. It represents the ultimate responsibility. My first task was to go to Dahlgren Naval Base for a refresher course on the Aegis weapon system. This time, though, my learning focus was on its employment from a command perspective. The folks at Dahlgren gave me every tool necessary to maximize the use of the combat system. Next, I traveled to Newport for Surface Warfare command school, brushing up on various Navy programs and regulations; I was also updated on changes that had occurred while I was on shore duty at the Pentagon. Finally, I headed to the command leadership school. I spent the first week by myself and then, was joined by my wife the following weekend on orders from the Navy.

Going Back to School

In my entire Navy career, this is the first time they issued orders for my wife to attend a school with me. This policy likely evolved from a famous study, which I read when I was a young officer on the

Biddle (bear with me – I'll eventually get to the value of spouses). I happened to see it on the wardroom table and took time to read it. It was about command excellence. The Navy wanted to know the difference between an excellent command and a mediocre command and the factors that contributed to both outcomes.

The number one cause of success of a command was "the Commanding Officer." *The lesson being that leadership matters a lot.* The number two factor was the relationship between the CO and his number two, the Executive officer also known as the XO. If that relationship is not solid, then problems will arise, and they will have difficulty solving them. The third factor is the relationship between the famous command Triad – The CO, XO, the Command master chief (CMC) for the Navy, also called Command Sargent Major (CSM) in the Army.

The lesson: Leadership is not just a singular activity but one of synergies between two (or more) individuals.

The Navy created the command leadership school to ensure high caliber CO's – the number one cause of command success. Next, it created an XO school as well and then, a command master chief school. All were part of the same organization, allowing the three leaders to intermingle and form a bond from the beginning.

I was polishing my command philosophy during this week at command leadership school. When my wife was with me in Newport, we took time to discuss this philosophy. The Navy determined in its study that the person with the most influence on a captain is the spouse. They discovered that the mood of a couple at home is reflected in the captain's behavior on the ship, and the mood that is established there. It was therefore crucial that a spouse understands what to expect and the challenges of commanding – and the spouse's role in helping a captain establish the right mood on a ship.

At the end of class, before graduation, husband and wife had to present their command philosophy in front of the entire class. We also received feedback and questions from the audience. This was a key moment, since it represented the last time your command philosophy is tested and questioned. Once you take command, your word becomes the law of the land. Perhaps you recall my earlier story of how my roommate wanted to take leave to go to a wedding, and the CO disapproved his leave just because of a scheduled inspection. The CO command philosophy was on his wall, and after he read it, my roommate said this guy is a hypocrite because his command philosophy emphasized how people come first before all, but he was putting an inspection first. There was a mismatch between what the captain said and what he was doing, and it destroyed the relationship between my roommate and the CO.

This is a lesson every leader needs to learn. There cannot be a say-do gap between what one says and what one does. It creates cognitive dissonance that makes people distrust their leaders.

There are literally hundreds of programs for which commanding officers are responsible. While they may have experts onboard running those programs, CO's must have a complete understanding of their intent and what they are supposed to accomplish.

As I've emphasized earlier, what the captain focuses on, the crew will be fixated on. Therefore, Captains should focus on the right thing; otherwise, they will lead the command astray. If they have a thorough grasp of all the programs being executed, they will be able to maintain the proper focus.

Assuming First Command

After a great deal of preparation, the big day arrived. I was to relieve my old detailer and friend as commanding officer. Typically, the new captain reports on Monday morning, and the turnover lasts about a week. I had a big briefing binder with the status of every program onboard. When I took over the ship, it was in the shipyard. On Thursday, we went to a hail and farewell, where the officers met me officially and said farewell to the outgoing captain.

At the gathering, I noticed that the officers clustered in various groups. On a ship where people come from many diverse backgrounds, people tend to congregate according to what they are used to.

We had the change of command on Friday at 1000 which is the Navy's customary day and time for a change of command. I started my change of command speech with one powerful word: "God." I said God is good and I thank him for being here today … and I made sure that my speech ended with this word as well.

My very first day in command of the Arleigh Burke was on Monday at 0700. As I approached the quarterdeck, the entire crew was in suspense wondering what the new CO was like – I'd been in their shoes. I walked onboard, and they sounded my new name for the very first time after the four bells – ding dong, ding dong "Arleigh Burke, arriving!" From that point on, I would take the persona of the ship: I was the Arleigh Burke. I represented the ship wherever I went. From the time I said at the change of command "I relieve you sir," until a new Captain relieved me, the command responsibility was mine, and nothing in the world can be used as an excuse for not being in charge. I was in command day and night, whether I was awake or asleep, on vacation, at home – I was always the Captain.

This is the definition of leadership. It means, as President Harry Truman once said, "The buck stops here." It is a complete acceptance of responsibility and a refusal to offer excuses or blame others.

I walked onboard escorted by the command duty officer just like I had done hundreds of times, starting with being a CDO in 1989 as a young division officer until 1997 in my last department head tour (XOs don't stand CDO watch). After I got my reports, I walked to the wardroom and made myself a cup of coffee and walked to my CO chair in my cabin. Next morning, when I came to my office, my coffee was already on my desk with two sugars, one cream – someone on the crew made it his business to know how the CO likes his coffee. It turned out to be the head mess attendant for the wardroom assigned to me, CS1 Gee. He came over and introduced himself. Everyone wanted to be of help. Everyone was ready to jump if I said jump.

I could see how power might go to some people's heads and suddenly, they convinced themselves that they were the best thing since sliced bread. Leaders need to resist the inflated egos that can result from being put in positions of power and create a false sense of infallibility.

In my first hour on the job, as I relished my perfectly made coffee and sat in my captain's chair, I contemplated being the Captain of a US Destroyer. I then pushed the chair away from my desk and spun around a few times – and that was my first action as CO, spinning on my chair. It was a simple, purposeful movement. It was designed to remind me that humility would guide me as I became the 9th captain of the Admiral's ship, the lead ship of an entire class of the most powerful warships in the history of naval warfare.

Shortly after coming on board, I had to tackle a delicate issue and set the mood for the ship. The week during my check in, I had learned that I had onboard a Jewish officer, a Muslim officer and the rest were mostly Christians. I spoke individually to the Jewish and Muslim officers. I told them that before each meal that we have together I would like to start by giving the blessing and asked if they would mind. They were fine with it. On Monday, my first day at lunch time, the officers gathered in the wardroom and the most junior officer onboard always in the surface navy designated as, "George," was sent to get me. I came in, stood behind my chair like the other officers and I said, "Let us give grace. Lord, we thank you for this meal and we thank you for this day. And we ask that You bless the officers, chiefs and crew of Arleigh Burke, Amen!" and then we sat and ate our lunch meal. No one said much. Of course, they would not. They did not know my conversation preferences. They deferred to the captain to set the mood for meals.

I understood that the first few meals and days would be crucial to my command. The tone I set would affect the wardroom and ship for the duration of my tour. For this reason, I suggested the

following exercise to the assembled officers: "I am happy to be
here with you as captain and I would like to know a bit about each
one of you. So, what I would like to do is for you to tell me two
things interesting about the person sitting on your left. I will start
first by telling you about the XO on my left." I said two things
about the XO, and the XO did the same about the CSO on his
left. The other officers, however, appeared puzzled, staring fixedly
at the person on the left as if they might read their minds to discover two things that they did not know.

I had assumed that the people in the wardroom did not really
know each other very well. Yet by the end of the evening, my
exercise had helped them relax and learn a bit about their fellow
officers. Before they left, I said that we would do the same thing
next week and that they had to sit next to a different person at
each meal. I also was aware that not all officers attended the lunch
(they're previously allowed to eat in their stateroom). I issued a
directive that all the officers be present at the wardroom for each
meal. Even if they do not want to eat, I said, they will join us and
sit on the couch and still partake in the conversation and fellow-
ship of our officers.

At the next meal, we had a full house. Everyone had a seat
around the table, and we proceeded to tell something new about
each person next to us. This time, they had prepared before-
hand. I started again with the very same prayer as before. Proper
naval etiquette calls for the senior officer to take the first bite
before any officer can start digging in, so I took that bite. We
had a nice meal, and each officer started conversing with others
at the table.

And then I told them that I would like to have entertainment
during meals. In the old days, the officers used to swap navy tales.
Based on that tradition, I asked that an officer volunteer to tell us
a story or a joke during the meal.

For this meal, I led off with a quick sea story. The next meal
I asked for a volunteer – a brave soul stood and told us a joke. I told

the wardroom that we should respond with a thumb's up or a thumb's down as to its quality. In this way, we could judge a story or a joke as a group rather than rely on my individual decision. On occasion, I added, I might override this group decision, but if I did, I would tell them my thought process and why I was overriding them.

In this way, I was setting the tone for our work and operation onboard the ship. I wanted the officers to make the right decisions, with me as an umpire. I wanted them to know and believe that I trusted them. This wardroom tactic helped me communicate this goal in a non-threatening, non-operational setting.

Leaders need to find a way to communicate indirectly. Relying on commands and statements gets across your message, but it doesn't always do so with nuance or resonance. Indirect messaging also helps people become accustomed to your preferences and goals, acculturating them in subtle ways.

I spoke with my senior watch officer and told her that after each lunch, I wanted an officer to stand and conduct training for a maximum of 15 minutes. This meant officer training daily, whether we were in port or underway. Topics could run the gamut – a description of a particular division, a piece of gear in the division, a process that was used successfully, or anything else. I got some push back from the SWO and the department heads; they believed that every day was too much. They recommended we do it once a week, but I did not give in. We had 33 officers, and I wanted them to each have a turn monthly. This way, the rest of the crew would learn a wide range of things from them, and each officer would have a chance to develop their presentation skills – skills officers needed.

I did the first post-lunch training. I discussed my perspective on being CO and how I came up with my command philosophy. I said that if I have to summarize my entire one command philosophy, it would be: "Be good, Do good work." I repeated those words for them, drilling it into their heads, since I wanted them to adopt this philosophy. Officer training daily after lunch soon became a welcome routine. We added a short Q&A afterward so people could request clarification or more information on a topic.

During my second week onboard, I asked the master chief to invite me to the chiefs' mess. I sat with the chiefs, we chatted, and at the end, I thanked them for leading the ship. I told them how important their jobs were and how much I believed in them. Then I made myself available for questions and insisted they feel free to ask me anything – no restrictions. And the chiefs went at it. Of course, I probably surprised the CMC with my approach, and I'm sure he was concerned his chiefs might embarrass him. My goal, though, was to make sure they knew that I understood and trusted them for who they were – I didn't want them to put on a different face for the CO.

We changed things up a bit in the coming months. For example, we rotated who gave the blessings. Before lunch, I would ask if anyone would like to say grace, and I'd usually get a volunteer. I also tweaked the storytelling/joke-telling format. I hoped to create an environment where everyone felt comfortable and part of the team.

Leaders build teams in all sorts of ways, and I believed that if I created an environment in which people felt trusted, informed and comfortable, the team building would follow naturally.

We also built teams through our "hail-and-farewell." These are the events hosted normally at the home of the captain when new members arrive or old ones depart. I held an offsite once a month with members of the wardroom. At first, they were all in my house and officers had a chance to relax, talk to each other, and make friends in a more social atmosphere. Then I started asking for volunteers to host these "hails-and-farewells." Building the team of Arleigh Burke took time; but it was something in which I was willing to invest energy and instill patience, since I knew the payoff would be huge and critical. Once we started our training cycle, stress and sweat entered the equation.

Training Philosophy and Practice

Running any large, complex organizations involves mastering many difficult tasks. It doesn't matter whether it's a corporation or a warship – a great deal of knowledge and skill is essential for them to run effectively. It's not surprising, therefore, that both enterprises invest heavily in training.

The training phase was divided by timeline. First, we did individual personnel training, focusing on the sailor to ensure that he/she knows the systems, understands the programs, and can operate the ship safely at sea and fight in a major war or a small ambush. Then team training focused on training the various teams aboard the ship. We emphasized damage control training, ensuring we could fight the various classes of fire from a small Charlie fire (electrical) to a major Bravo fire (lube oil of fuel oil). We also trained for the CBR (chemical, biological, and radiological) to ensure we could fight our way out of any situation. There was special training for the engineer team, emphasizing casualty control drills. We also did Combat information team training focusing on operation warfare and fighting with all the systems up and running. We engaged in integrated team training, confronting a battle problem that would stress all teams and every sailor onboard. Training regimens included a mass casualty drill, as well abandoning the ship, and rehearsing these procedures to ensure proficiency.

Training protocols weren't limited to our ship; we needed to train as a squadron where we worked with all our six ships. We would meet at the Virginia Capes area and start drills, practicing division tactics (divtacs), ship handling techniques that included difficult maneuvers.

One training that was not required by the Navy was the one I did in my captain's cabin. Every Thursday, when we were underway, I would gather all the officers not on watch in my cabin for my own training sessions. I would alternate using my battle orders – the captain's document guiding others on how the ship should fight – and the captain's standing orders, which included the night orders about how the captain wants the bridge to conduct the entire business of the ship while underway.

In nineteen years, on five different ships, I don't remember any captain doing this type of training – but I wish one of them had done so. No captain took the time to explain why he picked a certain piece of equipment or combat system setting or made a certain decision and what was behind this thinking. I never dared question COs about these matters; they would have thought I was either crazy or lazy.

When I became CO, I decided to explain to my officers what is in the book and why I do it one particular way. I had all the officers in my cabin, and I would rotate between the two documents (combat system doctrine: how the ship should fight and the captain's standing orders: orders to the bridge team), and I recommended that they each read the chapter before our session so I could answer their questions. I also warned them that I expected them to do the reading, would quiz them in front of other crew members, and ask them to explain certain aspects of the tactics or procedures. To avoid embarrassing themselves, I said, they should do the reading. I didn't want them to be embarrassed, but I hoped they would gain critical knowledge and bond as a team through this exercise. And most of them did.

One training protocol doesn't fit all. Leaders learn to adapt their approach to their particular preferences and goals. I wanted to train my people the way I wish I had been trained. By establishing my own "supplemental" protocol, I was able to help my officers acquire knowledge that would serve the ship and themselves well – and that they might not have acquired through traditional ways.

The Inspection

We had a board of inspection and survey scheduled – one that in the past had resulted in more than one captain being fired.

To prepare, we switched to preparation mode. We had two problems. First, we were working with a tight maintenance budget, and I couldn't obtain funding to repair a piece of equipment that required $200,000 to fix. Second, we had to have an immaculately clean ship, but to achieve this goal, we needed the engineers to clean up their areas, and they simply lacked the time to do so prior to the inspection – they were incredibly busy with repairs, and I didn't want them to take away from their repair time.

We devised a plan that was untraditional but necessary.

The best captains improvise with the material on hand. Situations sometimes arise where you're lacking the people, expertise or equipment to get the job done the usual way. Leaders think on their feet and employ creativity when best practices aren't possible.

After conferring with my officers and chiefs, we decided that since most division and other non-engineering work centers did not have as many gears as engineers, the cleanliness of their spaces was well in hand. Therefore, we decided to entrust the cleaning of the engineering spaces to other divisions and departments. This was unorthodox, but we were going into this inspection as a team.

Nonetheless, because of the challenges posed by our situation, I requested that the commodore postpone the inspection. The Commodore responded that the SURFLANT (Naval Surface Force Atlantic) Admiral said that I should do my job and if I could not, then I should resign and let someone else do it for me.

I was surprised by that response. Obviously, the admiral had become concerned when I requested a postponement. So concerned, in fact, that he scheduled a pre-inspection by my group commander admiral. The group Admiral would come aboard to determine my readiness for the formal inspection. I also received word that if I was not deemed to be ready or gave any hint of non-preparation, I could be fired.

We had a week to prepare. The day came, and I went to the quarterdeck to meet the admiral. I had all my officers posted in their assigned spaces. I told them I wanted the Admiral to see them doing the work, and how we did it. I also wanted the officers who were temporarily responsible for the engineering spaces to be the ones who were present rather than the engineering officers.

When the Admiral walked onboard, I greeted him warmly, but he did not seem to be impressed by my warmth. He abruptly asked me to take him to the wardroom. I escorted the Admiral there, gave him my captain chair and the gave the Commodore, the XO chair, on his left; I took the third chair on his right as the support chair.

Here is what the Admiral said: "Captain, I hope you are ready for this inspection. I want you to show me your top three spaces and your bottom worst spaces."

I requested that we start with my bottom worst spaces: after steering, after shaft alley, and auxiliary machinery two. He said okay but added that we shouldn't waste time and should get to work – he was a man on a mission whatever that mission was. I was calm and composed, confident that I was tackling the problem the right way given all the constraints I was facing, and the crew was 100% behind me.

As we walked to the first worst space, the Admiral had his game face on, looking eager to have himself a CO's behind for lunch. Perhaps he was assuming this mask because he did not want to do what duty may have required – firing a Captain is not an easy decision!

We opened the escape door leading to the very worst space on the ship: after steering. On most ships, this is a space full of hydraulic leaks and fuel smell, a space that not too many people go. It is normally not manned underway except during special situations like pulling into port or going into restrictive waters.

The Admiral entered the space and my young officer presented it with the utmost respect, confidence, and pride: "Sir, Ensign J, Fire control officer, presenting After steering." The Admiral was taken aback. What was a combat system officer doing in an engineering space? My officer told the Admiral it was his divisional duty to help the engineers while they were focusing on their drill sets, engineering program, and equipment repair. The Admiral paused and said okay, but I could see that the admiral was puzzled. My officer showed him the space, talked about the challenges he faced and how he overcame them with the help of his entire division.

The Admiral's attitude visibly changed. He was no longer looking at me like a lamb being led to the slaughter. He turned to me, offered a slight nod, and said he wanted to see the next worst space. We went down a huge shaft alley to observe a space that was normally a pigsty. My operation division officer presented her space and reported the space "standing by for inspection" (I had told them not to say "ready for inspection" as is customary navy procedure since I did not want to assume that we were ready to meet his standards). The Admiral conducted his inspection, and my officer spoke about challenges of the space and how we as a ship stood ready to tackle them before the big inspection.

The Admiral turned to me and said, "I was Captain of a Spruance Destroyer. My engineering space on the Spruance when I was a captain, it couldn't compare to yours. I could literally eat lunch on the deck of your shaft alley and after steering."

We eventually moved on to our top spaces. I suspected the admiral was satisfied by what he had seen, but I wanted a full inspection so that each officer had their chance to see the admiral and express pride in their work.

When we finished, the Admiral gathered with me and the commodore and my top leadership in the wardroom and told me that he has full confidence that Arleigh Burke will do okay in the inspection. Of course, he said it like it was a revelation, but it wasn't news for my XO, my department heads, my officers, my chiefs and my entire crew. We were confident that we were going to pass with flying colors – we never had any doubt in our abilities!

After the Admiral and Commodore had departed, I gathered my leaders in the wardroom and acknowledged their work. I also gathered the crew on the fantail and reiterated my full and absolute confidence in their ability to overcome anything coming our way. I told them that our hard training would make any fight a piece of cake and that we would be the ultimate judge of our success.

I went to my cabin for a few minutes to regroup with a cup of coffee and then, went back outside, walking the ship to be seen by my crew; they needed me to be there with them at the deck plate. Thinking about my approach, I recognized that I had deviated from tradition. But I had done so out of necessity, which truly is the mother of invention. I didn't copy my approach from a book or from a previous CO.

Leaders are willing to forge their own path, even if it's a path few if any have walked upon. It's risky to vary from the norm, but it's also situationally necessary in certain instances. Leaders trust their gut and their experience, and this trust usually pays off.

The day of the formal inspection came, and they informed me that they would be taking a very hard look at the ship. It was crucial that they do so because this particular ship was in its midlife. They wanted to know the status of every piece of equipment and use us as a benchmark. Every single one of the Aegis destroyers had run and would continue to run this inspection gauntlet.

The inspection was anticlimactic – we knew we would pass, and we did. But there was another major inspection yet to come.

Chapter 10

From Exercises to Exits

We passed the anti-terrorism and force protection inspections with flying colors, which gave our combat system and command duty officers a chance to shine. We had cleared the major hurdles, and we were ready for bigger and better things.

I focused a lot of our time and energy on training. In the past, junior officers had to go through a six-month division officer training course in Newport. I had done this, loved it and learned a lot. I was introduced to shipboard life and ship systems, making it easier to transition working on an actual ship.

But training protocols had changed. On the Arleigh Burke and other ships, the new officers would walk on cold turkey with the Navy expecting the CO to train the officers and then, they would go to Newport for two weeks of additional training.

One of my officers, Ensign Pete Furman, went to such a class. During his course, one instructor took a poll on shipboard officer training. The instructor asked class members to raise their hands if their ship didn't do officer training – a few hands went up. He then asked them to raise their hands if their ship did training once a quarter – fewer hands went up. Then he asked about once a week – again, a few hands went up. The instructor then addressed Ensign Furman and said you never raised your hand; what is going on aboard Arleigh Burke? Ensign Furman said onboard my ship, we do officer training every day.

The class was a bit taken aback, and they asked him how does one manage to do that? Pete explained that not only do we do officer training daily, we also have special training with the captain himself once a week in his cabin. The class was floored!

As I've noted earlier, I believed that good leaders make training a priority; that a well-trained crew is better prepared to handle whatever surprises occur at sea (and there are always surprises) than a crew not trained as well but with more personnel and more expertise.

Training might not be sexy, but it's what helps any group of people perform at a high level.

I valued great performance, and my crew knew and embraced this value. Here's one example. First class machinist mate, EN1 Navarra, had served for twenty years and had put in his retirement papers; we were all set to bid him farewell. The result of the chiefs' test came out around this time, however, and he had made the cut. EN1 was about to leave the ship forever when I had the chief engineer tell him to report to my cabin. I said, "EN1, I understand you are about to spend time with your family, and mentally transitioning out. How is that process going?" He said very well. I said, "EN1, I have an interesting proposition for you. I have the chiefs result in front of me and your name is in it."

EN1 Navarra was shocked! We talked about the impact of being a chief and we discussed the pros and cons of retiring and being with family. Then I told him that he was in a great position. He could either decide to retire or stay and become a chief. But I added that this should be a family decision. I told him to take two days off, go home to share the news with his wife, and discuss what they wanted to do. I said he should also seek guidance from friends, Chiefs, and his mentors. Two days later, he came back and told me he'd decided to stay on. I was happy for him; we rescinded his retirement package, and he became a Chief. It was a joyous day for both of us, the chiefs' mess, the crew, and the navy, because EN1 was a good man.

Leaders don't just train their people; they do everything they can to keep the people they've trained.

Putting What We Learned into Practice

We had reached an advanced level in our training, which meant we were ready to join the fleet and start working as a battle group. In our case, we got a special deal. NATO invited the US to be part of the NATO exercises in Scotland, so the US accepted and decided to send our squadron.

Around this time, a senior NATO officer told the second fleet commander that American surface warfare officers had become timid ship drivers. I thought the comment was probably justified. We had become so focused on being error-free that many captains were not willing to make mistakes because even minor mistakes could get them fired. Why take unnecessary risks if there was no need for it?

The second fleet commander sent us participating captains a message about being bold rather than timid ship drivers. That was a great recommendation, but the irony was that he failed to lead by example. He didn't say that he would forgive us if we make a mistake. Instead, he wanted to have his cake and eat it too – be bold, but if your boldness results in errors, you'll be punished.

Good leaders don't send ambiguous messages. Instead, they are clear about the behaviors and outcomes they value.

Our ships, as a squadron, would exercise together a week at a time, and the Commodore would push the envelope with us, and we all loved it. We developed a camaraderie within the squadron, and at sea we would practice division tactics until we got them down pat.

We would conclude our exercise in the waters around Scotland, and besides the Arleigh Burke, the other ships that would participate were Cruiser Anzio CG 68, and the destroyers, Winston S Churchill and Porter. An amphibious ship would also accompany us.

We got underway from Norfolk, and the Arleigh Burke was directed to proceed to the Bahamas for a day of special exercise to test the fleet entry of the MH-60R helicopter. We headed south, completed the exercise, and were directed to catch up with the rest of the ships in the Atlantic. I received a message to conduct an exercise as I joined the group. I was to conduct a WASEX – a war at sea exercise as a rogue ship. My job was to see if I could sneak in and attack the high value unit which would be the amphib. She was screened by the cruiser and two destroyers, and I was to come in and attempt to destroy her.

I gathered my war council, and we met in my cabin. We devised a plan and started to execute it as soon as we briefed the entire team. Though the tactic I employed remains classified, it helped us penetrate the group and kill the high value unit, sinking the cruiser and damaging both destroyers. The crew and the war council were extremely proud of this accomplishment. We were on top of our game. Then we joined the group and took our position and continued to Scotland.

Tactics matter. It doesn't matter whether you're employing military or business tactics, you need to be innovative, to think on your feet, to figure out what works in each situation. Great leaders are often great tacticians.

I weighed anchor at Greenock, a port not too far from Faslane, where the meetings were taking place. The next day, we all drove to have breakfast and meet our boss for the exercise. They had divided us in two groups. The American ships and the British Commodore on HMS Albion would be the rogue force against NATO. It is always more fun to be the bad guys in an exercise since you receive more latitude to use unorthodox tactics. The good guys usually must follow all the international rules and regulations but as a bad guy, you get to make your own rules. We met with Commodore Chris Parry, a fine British naval officer, and he told us about his philosophy of fighting.

Next, we met the rest of NATO. We had a big and heavy NATO book that our Operations officer had printed for us to review. I had my own personal Captain copy that I had read thoroughly to ensure I knew and understood all the NATO procedures and rules – there were a lot.

The exercise was a two-week event. We were to spend one week as a separate force and train by ourselves and then battle for the last week.

Again, I'm prohibited from detailing the various exercises, but by the end, I had developed great respect for Commodore Parry and his audacity and cunning wisdom. If ever I had to go to a real war, I would want to be on his team. We had a challenging one-week exercise and did things that an American admiral would never let us do in terms of rigor and risks. I executed a four-hour underway replenishment with a NATO oil tanker at sea under the most difficult circumstances – freezing rain.

Then the week came when the two forces would clash. It was a great week of training. We gave NATO the time of their lives trying to deal with four of the world's most sophisticated warships in the history of naval warfare. And they also gave us a lot of training. We engaged in all aspects of naval warfare during the week and time was divided into blocks. During a block of time, we would practice Anti-Air Warfare with focus on defense against incoming fighter attacks, bombers or missiles. Another period would be devoted to Anti-Surface warfare when we went ships-on-ships using the Harpoon Missile System. We also drilled on anti-submarine warfare, with various submarines involved in attacking us or us attacking them. We practiced Strike Warfare against land targets as well as electronic warfare, and several other non-kinetic ones as well.

We had developed a continuing-to-train mentality. For our upcoming deployment, the USS Arleigh Burke was designated to deploy as the US ship representing the United States to NATO as part of the Standing NATO maritime Group two (SNMG-2). NATO had sent another request for the next NATO exercise in Faslane and this time, they had picked two ships. Since the USS Arleigh Burke was designated to deploy as a NATO asset, the leadership decided to send the USS Arleigh Burke with USS Porter to this exercise. The exercise went well, and when we were done, we were offered the opportunity to stop at Rotterdam for some rest and relaxation. I presented this option to my crew, and they unanimously requested that we head home early rather than make a port visit. I did what they requested and we were home for Thanksgiving.

Leaders don't always have the opportunity or need to solicit their people's opinions, but in this instance, it made sense. We had just come off intense training exercises and had been at sea for a while, so it made sense to poll the crew. While leading an enterprise isn't always a participatory democracy, allowing everyone to have a say in certain decisions is wise. It's empowering, and leaders should do everything possible to make their people feel like they have an impact.

Up the Mississippi to New Orleans

After some time in homeport, some maintenance, and continued training, we received another assignment: a trip to Mardi Gras in New Orleans.

Driving up the Mississippi River was a challenge. I did not realize that the River was so big – enough for a warship to go up and space enough to meet up a large barge on the opposite side. We had a current of about 5 knots; each knot of current is equivalent to about 30 knots of wind on the side of the ship. Comparatively, there was almost the force of a hurricane on the hull of the ship down below. We arrived in port and met with the Chief of Police of New Orleans and said that the Navy was here to support the celebrations.

I was invited to go to the crowning ceremony of King Neptune. The emcee spoke and introduced King Neptune. King Neptune made his short speech, then VADM John Cotton as chief of Navy Reserve talked about the importance of the ceremony to the Navy and that we brought a warship as a supportive gesture. He introduced me. I was brief. I said on behalf of the Army, Navy, Air Force, Marine Corps and the US Coast Guard, I present you with a token of appreciation – the Arleigh Burke Ball Cap.

Ceremonies are valuable. Assembling groups of like-minded people in one place to honor someone or something – an accomplishment, a historical event – confers a sense of pride and builds community. After this ceremony, the Admiral invited a few of us to a reception for all the reserve admirals. We also provided them with a tour of our ship, and we had never had so many flag officers on the ship at the same time.

We were in port for a few days and gave the crew a chance to enjoy the celebration. Our crew had been working days and nights with long hours, and we decided to give them some rest and recreation. Prior to letting them go on liberty, I assembled the entire crew on the flight deck. I told them, "We are the Arleigh Burke, and we are here to be ambassador for the Navy and the Defense Department. We shall represent them well and we shall have a good time but there will be zero liberty incident."

We had a system in place called "yellow light and red light." If any sailor signaled a yellow light, it meant something was not right and the sailor needed to take some action to correct it: Either leave the place, stop talking, stop an action or whatever remedied the problem. If the same situation continued, then the red–light signal is given, which meant the person should return immediately to the ship. Anyone from the ship was allowed to give a red light to anyone else including chiefs and officers. If the sailor did not obey the red light and failed to return to the ship, then the sailor would voluntarily restrict himself onboard the next day.

Clear and unambiguous rules provide guardrails, whether on leave or on the ship. Leaders are responsible for creating, communicating, and enforcing them.

We had a great time in New Orleans for Mardi Gras and zero incidents. We left the day after Mardi Gras. It was quite challenging getting underway. We had another 4 knots of current, which meant we could not let the ships lines off. It was a tricky maneuver, in that the last line was still tied to the ship matching the speed of the river and after the line was let go, smartly bump up the speed to go forward and then, twist to go downriver. It was foggy, and it became a bit dicey as we were on a bend and another ship was coming up at the same time. Our watch team cooperated with CIC, and the entire team serving as lookout guided us through the situation until we reached clear and safe water in the Gulf of Mexico. We were to be the very last US Navy ship in the port of New Orleans before Katrina hit the city.

As we sailed away, I reflected on two additional incidents that occurred while we were there. First, at a dinner in New Orleans, my supply officer surprised me with a story. He said he went out to eat with his family, and to his own surprise, found himself saying to his family as they sat down to eat, "Let us give grace." Just like we had been doing on the ship, he gave grace to God and blessed his family meal before they all ate.

It struck me that life aboard ship has ramifications "offboard" not just onboard; that there are lessons learned such as the value of giving thanks that are applicable to countless life experiences. It reminded me that my words and deeds as ship Captain needed to be well-considered, since they might affect people I didn't know in ways I couldn't foresee.

One day, walking on the pier heading to the ship, I passed another destroyer that was docked. Then I heard the voice of a person calling to me. I stopped and turned around; it was a second-class petty officer. He said, "Captain, do you remember me? I am Seaman Ridenour, and I served with you on NICHOLAS when you were XO." I remembered him but was surprised that he was still in the Navy. "What are you doing back in uniform, I thought you had gotten out?" He said, "Yes sir, I did. I was nothing but a troublemaker when you were XO, and I was being discharged. You sat down with me in your XO stateroom and told me that even though I was being kicked out, it did not mean the end of the world. You said that if I put my mind to it, I could still continue serving in other capacities, that I could be anything I wanted, from the president of IBM to a senator."

"Those words went straight to my heart," Ridenour said. "After I got home, I looked for work and there was none. I went back to the recruiting center and asked to come back in and the Navy let me back in. I am now a second-class petty officer and was the sailor of the last quarter on my ship. I have been seeing you passing us since we pulled in. I just wanted to thank you for believing in me."

I wished him a great tour and continued success. Seeing him and how he'd changed made my day.

Sometimes, leaders have more of an impact than they realize. My words had stayed with Ridenour, had motivated him to do better. Sometimes, we underestimate how much of an impact we have on our people. A little encouragement can go a long way.

It was finally time to go on deployment. We had been training for almost over a year since our yard period, and we were ready to do our part in national security and defend our country and democracy.

Commanding a Small Armada

Since I was the senior officer in the task group, I was to be the Surface Strike Group Commander for SSG 06-1 and deployed with three ships: the USS Arleigh Burke the USS Porter, and the USS Carr.

Once we crossed the pond, I was to go to Greece to meet with
the Standing NATO Maritime Group two (SNMG-2). The other
two ships had their own requirements in the Mediterranean. All
three of us reported to Destroyer Squadron 60.

As the American ship assigned to NATO, I had two different
chains of command – US Navy admirals on the American side and
the NATO Admirals that I would meet up with in Piraeus, Greece.
The US Navy had not sent a ship to Greece for the last fifteen
years. The security situation was a bit tense. I was in touch with the
US Embassy and the Defense Attaché, and they briefed me on all
the threats and what to expect. It was a tricky situation since there
was no US Force presence to watch over me. I received a message
from the Senior US Navy officer in Europe and the Admiral was
very clear: If there was any incident whatsoever, the Captain of the
ship – that would be me – would pick up the phone and the first
person I would call would be the admiral himself and provide a
detailed description of occurrence: who, what, when, where, why,
and how. And now it was all up to me. The future was in my hands.

*Leaders are only as good as the people with whom they work. If we were
going to perform at peak capacity, it meant that I had to inform and inspire
my crew – everyone, not just my officers.*

I started with the most junior personnel on the ship, the E-1
through E-4 as a group. We assembled them on the mess deck. I
told them I had just received an email from the most senior
Admiral in Europe and basically, what he said was: "Captain, if you
screw up, you will personally give me a call and tell me what happened." I told my crew, "I believe in you as a team, and I believe
that you will take care of each other as you did in New Orleans.
If someone is going to mess up, I can almost guarantee that it is
not going to be from you, our most junior personnel. I know
most people are going to think that it will be one of you. I want
you to stand right here and right now and tell me if you think it
will be one of you or it is more likely to be a more senior person."
They all took the oath – it would not be any one of them who

screwed up. I said "Okay, I believe you. But if one of you messes up in port and I have to call the Admiral, rest assured that you will be standing right next to me, the XO, and the CMC, as I make the phone call. I want you to be there to hear and witness the Admiral's questions and my responses and it will be all because of you."

I went through this same routine with my senior petty officers and the rest of the crew and received their word that they would not screw up. I told the Chiefs and officers how shameful it would be for me to call the Admiral and have to defend a Chief or an officer's action in front of someone who is not even a crew member of the ship.

Shortly thereafter, we deployed to the Mediterranean Sea for six months. They knew that my time with them would end after this assignment and that I would move to another assignment after these six months.

It took us about ten days to get to Greece and when we moored, we met with officers from the nearby British ship HMS Manchester as well as nearby Spanish and Italian ships. When our crew was on leave, we continued to use our yellow light-red light system, and in this way, we avoided any incidents and also instilled the idea that we were all responsible for each other.

During our time in port, the US Ambassador to Greece and a very high official in the Greek military came to the ship to visit us. I gave him a personal tour, and during our stop in the Combat Information Center, I explained our command-and-control system. He looked at me and said, "How do you deal with so much power at your fingertips?" I responded without hesitation, "The more power at your fingertips, the more wisdom is required in your mind."

Leaders don't take their power for granted. They recognize that this is an enormous responsibility, and as such, they use it judiciously, intelligently and strategically – with wisdom, in other words.

Initially, there was a lot of meetings and dinners with captains of other ships that were moored nearby. Though some of this was social, we also discussed work-related topics – I focused our attention on the NATO handbook, since we needed to know and understand its terms, especially when we would schedule operations and the impact on various ships.

After one of these dinners, I returned to my cabin, and I heard the wind pick up. The Officer of the Deck started passing the word, mustering the duty section on the quarterdeck. The Command Duty Officer informed me that we needed to tighten the lines. I went to the bridge to look, then went down the quarterdeck as well. The wind was so strong that lines kept popping. Boatswain mates would go down and bring more lines but they kept popping off. I ordered the CDO to pass the word that everyone (whether they were on duty) should come out and give us a hand. We called port control, and they said the wind was so bad the tugs could not make it out to where we were moored; we were on our own.

I realized quickly that we were in a dangerous situation. We were boxed in with our port side at the pier and our bow, a few feet off the quay wall. On my starboard side, I had the British ship about 200 feet away, and the Spanish and German ships were right behind me. I did not have a chance to think about how they were doing and how they were dealing with this wind that came out of nowhere. My attention was focused on my own ship. I could not afford to have the ship break loose. If it were to do so, it would create havoc. Imagine a billion-dollar object with no power, bumping other equally expensive vessels. Suddenly the XO and the Chief Boats returned to the ship and jumped in to help. I did not trust the weather for the evening and our situation was sufficiently precarious that I ordered a tug to come and keep us pushed to the pier all night and only then, did I go to get some sleep.

The potential for disaster often arises seemingly out of nowhere – like that wind in Greece. You need to be prepared to take action without panic. You need to focus all your mental energy on the situation at hand. You need to figure out the optimal tactic for the situation. Not everyone can do this, but it's what good leaders learn how to do.

We finally got underway and started the NATO training exercises. We bonded as a maritime group with all the Captains getting to know each other. The Arleigh Burke was on top of its game. I had relieved a previous US ship in NATO, and we received a fresh batch of NATO ships in Rota Spain: the Dutch ship "De Ruyter," the German ship "Brandenburg," the British ship "Nottingham," the Italian ship "Aliseo." The CO of De Ruyter, Rob Bauer, whose call sign was, "Tango Papa," and I became great friends. He would later become the Chief of Staff of Netherlands and Chair of NATO Military Committee during the Putin invasion of Ukraine era. I also remained in contact with Simon Ward, CO of Nottingham, and Raimondi Giovanbattista, whose call sign was, "GeeBee," of Aliseo, as well as our German Chief of Staff, Mathias Metz.

We focused on our Mediterranean duties and our first port visit was Alexandria, Egypt. All the NATO ships pulled in, but I stayed in the Mediterranean "drilling holes in the water" – doing patrols while waiting for the other ships to come out on Monday morning.

During one of the exercises, near Crete, my crew detected a small vessel floating in the middle of the sea. We went to investigate and provide any necessary maritime support. It had a crew of about 7 people from various nations. We checked out their identification and it was a bit suspect. We were directed to board them which we did. This turned out to be exactly the 100th NATO boarding in the Mediterranean Sea. We turned them over to Turkish authorities to determine their intentions. We never really knew if we prevented a possible terrorist threat or if it was an illegal migrant crossing.

We Captains made the effort to get together when we weren't doing exercises. We recognized the value of getting to know each other as people, not just as captains. Developing relationships is not only satisfying on a personal level but facilitates more effective working relationships.

Each ship had its own culinary strength. Americans were known for good breakfasts, so we would have breakfast on the Arleigh Burke; the ALISEO had great coffee; the British ship provided excellent cold beverages while the Spanish ship was known for its exotic warm beverages. Through these visits for food and drink, we strengthened the bonds between us as nations and as seagoing officers, mariners.

Farewells

We had a penultimate port visit in Augusta Bay, Greece and my wardroom organized the most wonderful farewell of which a captain could have ever dreamed. All the officers gathered at the restaurant "Nykterida" also named "The Bat." We had a great meal together, and the owner brought me a taste of a special sherry and said it has been fermented for over twenty-five years! Then we transitioned to the official part of the farewell. The CSO, LCDR Monika Washington Stocker, and OPS LT Robert Blondin were in charge. They opened the floor and each officer had a chance to say a few words. Some thanked me for giving him or her the extra push to get to the top while others recounted a funny story or event that happened on my watch involving them. LTJG Dalton talked about his challenge passing the OOD board and how I pushed him to mental limits – a boundary he did not believe was possible for him to cross; Ensign Lee spoke of the warm initial officer get-togethers at the Captain's house; and LTJG Furman recounted his daily officer training story. Then the department heads and the XO had their say. They gave me a departing gift, a beautiful bell engraved with my name and that of the ship.

After some additional operations, we pulled into Palma de Mallorca for one more port visit before the change of command. The Command master chief and the Chief's mess decided to give me my own Chief's mess farewell. The CMC told me that the first evening in Mallorca belongs to the chief's mess and their captain – I said I was perfectly ok with that.

After taking care of some final bits of official ship business, I changed to civilian clothes and the CMC and another chief picked me up in a car and they drove me to a hotel. I checked in, relaxed and was requested to come down around 7:00 p.m. for dinner. But I went downstairs before then and saw some of the chiefs starting to assemble with the CMC in a nice common area of the hotel. I joined them, we started talking and for the first time, I was made to feel like one of their very own rather than their boss – they treated me like a fellow chief, with dignity and respect. Now, I cannot and would never pretend to be a chief since I had not put in the work and training their positions require. But we broke bread together, and each chief had a special word of wisdom to share with his about-to-be-former Captain. The CMC finished up with some final words of wisdom and a souvenir to remember them by. I was so happy to be with my chief's mess. We had been through so much together and each one of them knew exactly how I felt about them.

Captains can't be one of the guys. To a certain extent, all leaders are alone at the top. But that doesn't mean we can't appreciate and value our people. I knew every one of the chiefs well, and though we couldn't be buddies, we could like and respect each other. Leaders need to know their people well and establish strong working relationships where bonds are built.

We began the last voyage to the last port where I would have my change of command and turn the ship over to another captain. Prior to pulling in, the crew invited me to the mess deck and gave me their own farewell. Without my knowing it, the crew had taken pictures of me throughout deployment that were on display now. They played a video of the Arleigh Burke, leaving Norfolk, going on deployment and showed various events and how I was running things. Designated members of the crew of various ranks came up to the front and said their own farewells. I was moved and appreciative. In my twenty years at sea and on six different ships, I'd heard a lot of stories about how captains departed, but I'd never heard of anything like this. I had a special relationship with my crew. For the last twenty-five months, they were my world, and I was their leader and they trusted me with their lives. And they also knew that if the ship were in trouble, I would have been the last to leave. They understood my commitment to them and the ship.

We pulled into Malta the following day. I got off the ship as they were still tying it in. I wanted to see the crew in action one more time as Captain. I left and Ops went with me. There was a restaurant right on the pier and we grabbed a cappuccino and watched the ship tying up. It was a beautiful and powerful sight. Rob Blondin, my Ops, asked if there was anything else I would like to do before I depart as captain. I responded, "absolutely nothing!" I did all that I had set to accomplish. Before I took command, I had my top twenty-five things to do list. I did not wait until the last minute to do those things and accomplished all of them during command. I had no regrets.

I know there are leaders who have regrets when they depart. They wish they had made acquisition X or would have expanded into market Y. What's satisfying about being a top leader is the opportunity to turn your vision into action. While no one has carte blanche, leaders usually possess sufficient clout to do what they want within reason. Yes, everyone is answerable to someone — a board of directors or admirals. But leaders who play it too safe — who fail to seize the opportunity to explore, to innovate, to take risks, to make changes — will leave their jobs feeling like they missed an opportunity.

As I bid farewell to the maritime group, most of the captains wanted to pull in their ships near mine and participate in the ceremony, but the Commodore decided that they should stay out at sea.

Every morning underway, at reveille, since I reported aboard, the Officer of the deck would pick a song to play after reveille was passed. First the whistle then the words: "Reveille, reveille, all hands heave up and thrice up. Breakfast for the crew." I let the crew decide on the song rather than the Officer of the Deck. My very last morning underway, waking up to pull into Malta, the OOD played the very last song for me. As I heard the whistle and woke up, on the 1MC announcing system came one of my favorite songs, "My Way," sung by Frank Sinatra dedicated to their departing captain. I stayed in bed as I listened to the entire song. I felt so good – that was a perfect choice by the OOD and for me. We got some breakfast in the wardroom, the officers not on watch were with me and we celebrated our last meal as a crew together. Soon, at the entrance of the channel, we would pick up the new Captain. After we picked up CDR Esther J. McClure, we let her drive the ship a bit prior to pulling into the port. It was my job to make her feel welcome and at home in her new ship and command.

After the ship finished docking, I was interviewed by newspapers and a television station on the port bridge wing. My family arrived during the interview, and I waved to them, and the reporters asked me about my family and the hard deployment away from them. I told them about our sacrifice and what it takes to support and defend freedom and our liberties.

The next morning, I met with the new Captain and answered her questions about various issues. After the meeting, I sat on the Captain's chair of the port bridge wing watching the crew rehearse for the upcoming change of command. I got to thinking about the crew. There were all type of performers – from superstars to low performers, from officers who were future captains to crew members who were troublemakers. No matter who they were, though, they were all my crew. Being captain of a ship meant being the CO for everyone – even the troublemakers.

The day came to turn over the Arleigh Burke to another captain. On Thursday, the crew, including both incoming and outgoing Captains, had a dress rehearsal on the quarterdeck, the actual location of the event. On Friday, a buzz of excitement ran through the ship. At 1000 sharp, the event started with the XO, LCDR Dino Pietrantoni, welcoming everyone and telling them about the meaning of the change of command in the US Navy. The US Ambassador to Malta was present, as were various dignitaries from Malta and the media. I chose the guest speaker to be Captain Tom

Daniel who was then serving on the staff of 6th Fleet in Naples, Italy. Tom was ops officer on my very first ship USS Biddle as we were the only two out of thirty-three officers of African descent onboard. Everything went smoothly, and I passed command to the new Captain per Navy tradition.

My tour as CO of the most powerful warship in the history of naval warfare came to an end. I enjoyed every day, even the low points. I enjoyed my crew, and I enjoyed my ship. Nothing I had ever done before or after comes close to what it means to be a Captain of a US Navy warship at sea! It is best described by the Joseph Conrad poem in "The Cruel Sea"; he referred to it as "the burden of command."

It's a burden that leaders bear wisely and fully. At times it is a joyous burden, at times a challenging one. It may cause sleepless nights, but it also invigorates. Whether you're in charge of a ship or an organization, you are given a sacred trust – people are looking to you for direction, for praise, for constructive criticism, for desired outcomes. It a huge responsibility, but good leaders embrace it and treasure the opportunity to be at the helm.

Chapter 11

Teaching in School, Training in War

I returned to Virginia Beach in the Spring of 2006, took a few days off and then, arrived at my next duty station: Command Leadership School in Newport, Rhode Island. This is where I chose to be, where the Navy sends its most senior officers heading for command positions. It is a highly-focused, two-week session dedicated to leadership at the most sophisticated level.

I reported to my new command at the school. When I arrived, the first person I saw was Captain Ed Boorda, the school director and the son of the former CNO Admiral Mike Boorda. I introduced myself as the new member of the team. Oddly, Captain Boorda's welcome was somewhat cool, and I would only understand the meaning of that moment a few months later.

Passing on What I had Learned

Command leadership had six different classes going on at any one time, and I was teaching the PCO class for senior officers going to their first commands. Commander Mike Hammer, a submarine post CO, oversaw the overall course. He scheduled the class and

163

determined who would teach what topics. The first morning of class on Monday at 0800 for me was the best class. The students were a mix: surface warfare officers, submarine officers, aviators of all the types of aircraft flown by the Navy, Navy SEALS, explosive ordnance officers (EOD), medical Seabees and others. Their varied backgrounds and experiences make the course interesting and instructive for all officers attending.

The first morning lecture was RAA – Responsibility, Authority and Accountability. I remember teaching that first morning course, and I would start with "Navy regulations Article 0802: The commanding officer has absolute "Responsibility" of his command (probably the only place in the US Government where the word absolute is found)." Then the regulation adds that the commanding officer has enough authority to discharge one's absolute responsibility but stopping short of giving anyone in command absolute authority over any American military person. If one thinks that one needs more authority, then one must ask for it from above. The final A is for Accountability. Every commanding officer will be held accountable for his or her actions or failure to discharge one's responsibility.

I was also a lecturer/facilitator for a PXO class that ran concurrently with the PCO class. It was for Executive officers heading to their XO tour. The third class given simultaneously was for the Command master chiefs.

These three classes form the triad of command in the US Navy. They all involve participation around case studies and require the officers to play their actual roles: A Commanding officer would play the role of captain; the XO would play the XO and the CMC would play CMC. Together, they would come up with solutions to various problems and present to them during case studies, relying on the Harvard Business School case study method.

Earlier, I discussed a 1985 Navy study on command excellence, and the study found that three factors impact command performance: the quality of the commanding officer, the relationship between the CO and XO, and the relationship of the CO, XO and

CMC to each other. Given this study, it makes perfect sense that the Command School offered courses for the CO, XO and CMC. As you may recall, this study, also found that spouses have a significant influence on job performance – that's why they're also invited to participate in a class at the school.

Another study found out that most mistakes made by navy commanding officers were not by first time commanders but by commanders in their second command. We were then tasked by the chief of Navy personnel to put together a one-week refresher course for the senior captain going to their second command. Captain Boorda assigned that task to me, and we created a rough curriculum that was reviewed and accepted by senior Navy leadership. Both of us partnered to teach the course together.

Another Navy study prompted us to do diversity training for prospective leaders. We hired a consultant who gave us one-week diversity training, and as part of the exercise, each of us discussed our biases. We were all very open. Captain Boorda candidly admitted that he was unaware of his own prejudice. He said the day he met me, without even knowing me or my credentials, he thought, "Well, here goes my token Black guy." After he admitted the bias reflected by this comment, he apologized to me and said that was not deserved because I proved myself to be as qualified as any of his other officers teaching courses. We all learned about ourselves through this training, and we were all ready to teach the course. I was paired with another captain, and we orchestrated a marathon session at first with everyone at the same time – PCO, PXO, and PCMC. Some of our diversity discussions got heated since these folks were not used to frank and open discussion about race and prejudices. Despite disagreements at times, the class was valuable in that it raised everyone's awareness about their prejudices.

I tried to bring biases out in the open rather than allow them to fester beneath the surface. This can be a difficult, uncomfortable task for a leader. But it's absolutely necessary, since many biases are unconscious and can be managed when people become aware of them.

To sharpen my leadership skills, I went to the Naval Academy to attend a one-week leadership course. I took a battery of psychometric and leadership tests, including Meyers Briggs, 360-degree feedback, and so on. I became certified as a 360 instructor and provided the psychometric and leaders test to others.

Soon after reporting to Newport, I applied and was accepted into the Doctoral program at Salve Regina University. I would be a teacher in the daytime and a student in the evening and weekends.

Even the best, most experienced leaders embrace continuous improvement. There is always something more to learn, and I was intent on adding to my working knowledge of how to lead.

From School to a Combat Zone

It was my time to go to an Individual Augmentees assignment. For me, this meant helping to fight the global war on terrorism. The Navy sent officers and enlistees to help the Army and the Marines. My assignment was to be Iraq.

I took a flight to Norfolk, and my wife got a special pass to escort me all the way to the gate. We stayed together until my Iraq flight boarded. I could not imagine what was going on in my wife's head – or the mind of any Navy spouse whose husband or wife is about to deploy to a war zone. I was ready because the Navy had trained us to be warriors, but no one had trained our spouses! As much as I was going to miss her, I coped by focusing on the mission to come. I was wondering how I was going to make a difference. I just had to learn, assess and see where I would make my contribution. The whole time on the flight, I was thinking about Iraq and re-reading my briefs, the US mission in country, the global war on terrorism, why we were there, and the overall mission. I was laser-focused!

I arrived at Norfolk's Naval Military Processing Unit (NMPS) and was welcomed by a Navy commander of NMPS. Next, I visited the Expeditionary commander readiness center (ECRC), Capt. "Spuds" McKenzie and I received a brief of the area and the operation. During the time in Norfolk, we obtained our uniforms and all our gear for the desert, including the brown camouflage uniform.

During one stop at the Navy exchange, I was having lunch when I was approached by a young Petty Officer. He introduced himself and said he had served on the Arleigh Burke. He explained that he wanted to thank me. He told me he had given up on himself while on the Arleigh Burke – he'd had a series of problems that got him in trouble – but he told me that I'd never given up on him and had given him second chances. He said my support had renewed his faith in himself, and that he'd done well in recent months, even receiving the "Petty Officer of the Quarter" once.

These moments make me feel very proud about our Navy and the difference a leader can make in someone's life. When you're the leader of a lot of people, you don't always see the impact you make in an individual's life. Every so often, however, incidents like this one occur, and it reinforces the belief that leaders make a difference.

During this time, I kept reviewing my briefings and the job I was about to tackle in Iraq as the Navy Officer in charge. A bus took us from Norfolk to Fort Jackson in South Carolina. It was just like being in boot camp all over again. We met with our physical training instructor who arranged us in a platoon, and we lined up by squad. I learned that a line of three was a platoon and one line comprised a squad. In the Navy, we don't do squad or platoons – it was literally a new language for me. I enjoyed the physical training starting with exercise, stretching and calisthenics coordinated and done in a disciplined Army way. It was my first introduction to Army training and the Army way of thinking.

We had two weeks of training at Fort Jackson and still had no clue what to expect on the other side. The other side was like a black hole. You just go through your training, don't ask anything, assuming that when you need to know something, someone will let you know. This seemed to be the Army way. Which is completely different than the way the Navy operates. In the Navy, the commanding officer keeps the crew appraised of operations so they can be mentally prepared for what is to come. In this new world, I felt like a sheep being herded and not knowing where my next step would be.

The training, though, was excellent. We had training on shooting synthetic and live ammunitions. They gave us various and realistic scenarios. They showed us what to do in a rolling Humvee, and how to get out. We also went through excellent survival training. I loved every minute of it.

During our last exercise prior to deployment, Captain MacKenzie, who was the officer sending me to Iraq and someone that I greatly respected, had the OIC pull me out of class and requested to speak with me immediately. My first thought was that something has happened to my wife or family – pulling someone out of an exercise was unusual. Fortunately, it was nothing like that. Instead, my orders had changed. I was being sent to Kuwait and not Iraq. It turned out that Admiral Masso and the IA Task Group wanted to consolidate the entire Navy IA operation in the Middle East and make me Task Group commander in-country, having all the other captains report directly to me; I would report to ECRC as the commander in charge. My mind was spinning; I had to shift my thinking and orient to a completely new assignment–the Captain assured me that I would figure everything out when I reported to duty.

The ability to pivot is crucial for people in positions of authority. Especially in the volatile world in which we live, work and fight, situations shift rapidly. In business and in the military, agility is essential. Instead of complaining and feeling sorry for yourself, you need to shift your thinking on a dime. "Bloom where you're planted" is a good adage for leaders to live by.

We took a chartered flight to Kuwait, and as we flew over the Middle East, I noticed the fire shooting out of the oil chimneys below us, as well as the expanse of ocean. As we got closer to Kuwait, the ground was a foggy brown. There was a permanent sand cloud covering the earth.

We landed at Ali Al Saleem Airport; a monster of an airport operated by the US Air Force. And then we waited … and waited. A half an hour became an hour became a number of hours. As one of the senior officers aboard, I went to inquire about what was going on. I found out that the Navy folks in country were there to pick us up but couldn't do so until the Kuwaiti escort vehicle showed up. How long would that be? They didn't know.

Day became night and still nothing. Finally, the Kuwaiti escorts showed up. One member of the Navy team escorted me down the steps. As soon as I went outside, I was hit by a heat wave that I had never experienced before. The temperature was over 110 F.

The Captain I was relieving picked me up with his own car, and we headed to Camp Virginia in Kuwait. It was dark, I could not really tell where we were and where we were going. We finally arrived at the office, a tent on the north end of the base. The captain left me, and I took that time to walk around the large tent. Eventually, everyone else arrived and it was midnight when we were told to head straight to the auditorium; basically, another tent with room for 300. We were welcomed aboard by the Senior Chief and watched a short video where the Army General in charge of Kuwait welcomed us.

I questioned the efficacy of such timing since everyone was dead tired and was in a daze in a foreign land in a war zone with no clue of what was going on. Whatever the general on the video tried to convey, no one absorbed it. As a member of the Kuwait team, I was assigned a small temporary room next to the tents and shown the common latrine and shower areas. I was told to wear shoes going outside at night since there were scorpions in the area. I was told that they shine under a black light, but I had no access to such a luxurious item. Before going to bed, I said my prayers and gave thanks to God for bringing me safely to the war zone and being with me always.

In the middle of the night, I awoke and looked up, and saw in the distance, a red light that resembled a twinkling star at its zenith. I also saw a green star rising on the far distant horizon. I stared in confusion at these two lights for a few minutes since I had seen this same scene before in a dream when I was in Virginia Beach. It was a strange and weird coincidence. As I awoke fully and my eyes got used to the complete darkness in the room, I realized that the lights weren't outside but the glowing bulbs on the room's air conditioning unit. Still, the parallel with my earlier dream combined with my current misperception spooked me. I was in a different world from the one to which I had become accustomed.

The alarm awoke me and after taking a shower, I noticed that the sleeping area was blockaded with huge security and safety brick walls. I crossed over the sand road and arrived at the breakfast area. The food was varied and superb; the Army is an expert in humongous logistics operations. Hands down, they had this figured out quite well. I looked for the Navy uniforms and went over to sit with our Navy folks; birds of a feather flock together. Then we headed over to another area and received additional briefs.

One brief was delivered by a young medic. He was telling us about the safety procedures and what to expect over the next couple of days. For some reason, though, he was peppering his talk with what I thought of as Drill Instructor words—obscenities. We were a group of about 350 ranging from senior Captains to a few young Petty Officers. As the young medic continued, the other captains seemed confused and uncertain about what to do about this inappropriate speech; they started looking at me, knowing that I would be the new guy in charge of this operation. I had to do something. I told the head medic to stop his young medic and let us take a bathroom break. HM1 did as instructed and during the break, ordered the young medic to stop using off-color language.

Taking action in uncomfortable or confusing situations can be challenging. I thought I was there just to listen but instead had to deal with a minor but troubling situation – you can't let your people act inappropriately. I found a way to accomplish this task without embarrassing the young medic, which was also important.

Then it was time for me to assume command from the captain who had been in charge. I had a solid grasp on all the operations and logistics of the command. After two days, everybody came back from their advanced weapons training, and I went to greet them. We had a convoy to take them to the airport in Ali Al Saleem. They were divided in groups going to Afghanistan and Iraq. The airport was a huge operation, and our Air Force pilots flying the "heavies" were highly professional and skilled young officers. It was a massive operation, and it unfolded smoothly.

One of my first actions in command was to write a letter to the very next incoming class. It started like this: "Good morning, I am Captain Charles Stuppard and like you, I am an IA and attended Fort Jackson. I want to give you an idea about what to expect after you depart Fort Jackson on Friday. It will be a long flight, but the food is good, and it is all free. When you get to Kuwait and exit the plane, there will be a very big temperature difference, and you will experience a new meaning of the word, 'heat'. There may be a delay picking you up as we cannot depart without a Kuwaiti escort. But know that we are there outside awaiting your arrival. You will be tired but will have time to catch up on sleep later. You will spend about 4 to 5 days in Kuwait to acclimate while we provide you with additional training. Afterward, we will get you on your way to your destination where another Navy captain will ensure that you arrive safely to your assigned unit. I am looking forward to seeing you when you get to Kuwait."

Leaders set expectations. Uncertainty and confusion are demoralizing. It doesn't take a lot of time or effort to help people understand what will happen, and it pays off in gratitude and confidence.

After the new class arrived, they assembled the next morning in the big tent auditorium. They each found their place to sit. When it was time, I entered from the main door in the rear. Someone called "attention on deck" and everyone stood at attention. I immediately called "at ease". I wanted to remind them of the intense discipline required in the war zone and that was instilled in all of us when we first joined the Navy but not to an extreme level. It was a balancing act.

After greeting them, I asked for feedback about my letter and their responses were positive. Then I told them, "Welcome to Kuwait." I also gave them a very brief overview about the next few days and stated that my staff will go over the details with them; that I had a captain in Afghanistan and one in Iraq who work for me and that these two captains will ensure they get to where they are supposed to go.

And then I made them a promise. I said that if at any time they have a problem or an emergency that their captain couldn't resolve in 48 hours, they should call me. I gave all of them my personal number at the office. I said, "You call me, and I will take care of your issue. If I must find you, I will fly to your country and wherever you are, whatever rock you are under, I will come and get you." And they saw the seriousness of my face – I was not kidding or making an empty promise. This was a promise on which I would deliver.

Leaders have their people's backs. It's not just words. Brilliant generals, CEOs, politicians and others demonstrate their support with action. If you want your people to go the extra mile for you, you have to go the extra mile for them.

After the brief, I invited all Captains and all Master Chiefs to have lunch with me. During lunch, I made myself available to answer questions they had. I also invited them to share any sea story – it was a great way to build bonds among senior Navy leaders. Lunch and sharing stories gave me a chance to meet the other leaders in the class and start developing relationships.

I cannot overemphasize this point: Relationships matter. In the "old" days, some leaders were above it all, issuing commands from on high. Relationships not only create loyalty and engagement, but they are gratifying for all involved. They also make it more likely that you receive honest feedback.

Challenges

One of my Captains slipped through the cracks – he arrived and departed for Iraq without going through training under my auspices. This was more than a little troubling.

My task was to ensure everyone received critical survival training before they went to the war zone. I contacted my team leader in Iraq and got in touch with the captain. I told him about Navy requirements, that he needed to return and receive necessary training. It turned out that this Captain had slipped through the cracks because the group he was going to work with in Iraq had expedited the process to get him in country as soon as possible; they weren't aware of the training protocol. I was concerned that he could get injured or killed because he lacked the necessary training to defend himself. I would not be able to live with myself for such a failure of duty. Fortunately, after explaining my rationale to the Captain, he understood and returned to undergo training.

I wanted to prevent such miscommunication from reoccurring. I briefed my boss about this situation, and he asked for help from another fellow captain working with the Army leadership in Kuwait. I emphasized that the help I needed was from the folks in country, not in Kuwait. The chain of communication was extremely complex, but I understood it. Fortunately, such an incident never happened again.

The lesson learned is that at a certain level of operations, you may see something that others do not see. It is then your duty to flag it and ensure people higher up see and understand your concerns. Sometimes, the issue isn't obvious, and it's your responsibility to call attention to it.

A new challenge arose in Afghanistan. A captain there emailed and spoke with me about his concerns that his people were going to town to engage with Afghanistan leaders using regular SUVs. He kept telling me that his people were not safe. He feared that they would be the victims of IEDs and said they needed up-armored cars.

I was not operationally in charge of the Navy folks in country but I felt that as a senior officer in the Navy, if there was a problem and it was not being addressed, then my duty was to either address it or ensure someone was addressing it. I informed my ECRC boss in Norfolk of this issue; he addressed it with Fleet Forces command, and they issued us six up-armored Humvees for our folks to do their job.

When I heard this, I felt obliged to inform another senior officer in Bahrain to whom I reported about receiving these vehicles. He then sent an email to his other commanders in country and said he had six Humvees arriving and did any of their units need any.

I was furious! I was responding to a specific captain's request, and now my superior officer was trying to capitalize on the six Humvees that I had put into play. It turned out that this officer distributed the Humvees to a variety of captains, not just the one who had contacted me. The incident created a bit of friction between my boss in country (who had distributed the Humvees) and the one back in the States. Who was my "ultimate" boss? The lines of command weren't clear. What I did care about was which boss would be more responsive and care more about the issues I raised.

I ended up flying to Afghanistan to visit the captain who had requested the Humvees and figure out how I could help him address the other issues that concerned him and how I could best support him and his team.

It's not always possible for leaders to be fair, but fairness is something to strive for. In this instance, I had to accommodate my boss, thwarting my efforts to supply the captain with the vehicles he needed. But my visit to Afghanistan helped restore at least some fairness to the situation, giving me the opportunity to help him deal with other problems.

In the next few months, I had a series of experiences that helped me learn and grow as a leader. I was thrust into new and unfamiliar situations, and I met a series of inspiring leaders. For instance,

I traveled to Iraq on a special VIP jet because I had a Navy two-star Admiral with me, RADM Sonny Masso. He was at Navy Personnel command and in charge of all Navy personnel going to the war. He wanted to get a feel himself for how things were going. His visit coincided with the pinning ceremony of our Navy chiefs in Iraq. During the CPO pinning, General Petraeus was present. He was very well respected by all of us since he had done such a fabulous job. He had been in country for over four years, away from his family for this extended period of time.

I also went to visit a Navy Commander who was in charge of the Navy team running the largest prison in the world – Camp Bucca held over 22,000 people then. The prison was divided into three zones. The white zone was for those people who were not too dangerous, and the US Air Force oversaw that section. The next zone was designated as yellow and had a bit more dangerous people in there, and the US Army oversaw them. The next zone was red where the most dangerous prisoners were detained. It was divided into a fenced square which in turn was subdivided into four inner fences with 250 people within each inner square – a total of 1,000 prisoners per large square. The Navy oversaw five such squares for a total of about 5,000 prisoners.

I went inside one, checked in with the guard and spoke with the prisoners. Most spoke English very well. I asked one guy why he was there. He told me that he was a translator for a team in Baghdad and an IED exploded and the Americans believed that he was responsible for giving away their position – they thought that he was a spy for Al Qaeda. He tried to convince me that he was not, that we had made a mistake. I said that a process existed for him to plead his case when it was his turn. Another prisoner informed me that when he was freed, he would not go back to Baghdad. After his release, he wanted to go to Switzerland. He explained that he wouldn't return to Iraq because he was a member of the Saddam Hussein intelligence group, and that the Iraqis would hang him if he went back.

During the whole time in country, I continued to work on my PhD. For me it was an outlet. Something to clear my mind and take me away from the war zone. One moment I would be confronting the death of our military men, and in the evening, I would be reading about Heidegger and his perspective about thinking!

Part of my job was to take care of all the people under my command. War is insane, and to maintain our sanity, I made sure that people got together often and developed relationships. In the evening, we would all gather at the volleyball field under the bright lights when temperature would go down to the 90's, and we would play volleyball and tell sea stories or just talk. It was a way to be together and encourage each other. It was a better option than staying in your tent by yourself and dwelling on how much you missed families and friends. We built a tight group where we provided strong moral support for each other.

Sometimes, the best thing leaders can do is focus on the humanity of the individuals in their charge. It's not glamorous like giving a rousing speech or intellectual like designing a brilliant strategy, but it's necessary and valuable. Providing regular opportunities for people to speak and interact can go a long way to achieving this goal – helping people help each other.

The Transition Challenge

At Camp Arifjan, I had a Submarine Navy LCDR who was pushing hard to find a place for our Warrior Transition Program. It has been in the works for some time, and he was getting a lot of push back from the Army. He was fully dependent on another Navy group, Navy Expeditionary Logistics Group (NAVELSG), to do the warrior transition program, and they helped us out. My Command Master chief and I tried to convince the Army installation commander and his deputy to let us build a navy tent for this unique program. What followed was a lot of negotiation. Finally, though, we received the go-ahead.

I realized how important it was to help soldiers and sailors transition from a war zone to peacetime service. In fact, I now understood that returning home was a much bigger challenge then going to the war zone. In the former instance, soldiers were well-trained and pumped up. Returning was a challenge. How do we reverse the process and send people back home mentally and spiritually safe?

We created a team designed to answer that question for our Navy IA's, composed of military chaplains and social workers. It became clear to me that I needed to move to Camp Arifjan full time to focus on the warrior transition piece.

I notified my boss in Bahrain that I was moving down south to the Camp. His response made my jaw drop: "Are you moving to Camp Arifjan from Camp Virginia because they have better food and bigger housing?" I was flabbergasted and heartbroken. I would have given my life for the folks under my command, and this Navy captain was suggesting I was doing it for personal gain.

Leaders need to develop thick skins and do what they believe in their mind and heart is best to achieve the desired goal. People are always going to snipe and second guess. You need to be prepared to take some hits. But if you go with your gut – if you do what you know is right – then any criticism can be endured.

I had the best interest of my team in mind. I would not be deterred, and I pressed on with my plan!

We constructed the Warrior Transition Tent and named it the "Murphy" Tent for the first one of our fallen sailors in combat. I remember that I wrote a letter to Mrs. Murphy, which was one of the hardest letters I had to write! What can you say to a spouse whose husband went to war and was returning via Dover Air Force Base.

The warrior transition process took about five days. Our sailors would arrive from Kuwait or Afghanistan to Kuwait. We orchestrated the entry process to begin the transition effectively. Each person arrived at the tent and was asked to deposit their helmets, breast plates and protective gear in a bin. We wanted people get rid of all their war gear first thing. In the afternoon, we had a weapon cleaning station in which everyone must clean their M-14 or M-16 and the 9MM pistol. After it was fully cleaned and inspected by one of our guys, we took custody of them. The next morning, they all come back after breakfast for the first set of briefings which normally last two to three days. Then we bus them up back to Ali al Saleem to Kuwaiti airport for a rotator civilian jet to take them back home.

One day after the weapons cleaning, a young LCDR knocked on my door and requested to speak with me. He told me that he was a F-18 fighter test pilot stationed at Pax River, in Maryland. He had made over seven deployments on aircraft carriers to Iraq and Afghanistan and said he didn't require this transition process. He requested that I immediately get him home on a civilian flight. I asked him about his assignments and how it went – it had been a grueling experience. I suggested that the class would benefit greatly from his presence and participation in the briefings. I requested that he stay not for himself but for his shipmates. He agreed and left. Late the next day, the same LCDR came to my office and asked to speak with me again. He said, "Captain, I came here to apologize to you. After I left you, I went to the gym, then grab some food, sent out a few emails and went to bed by 8:00 p.m. I slept until 8o'clock the next day for twelve hours. When I awoke, I went for a quick run and then had breakfast, got dressed, went to the briefings and now I feel so good. I have been going at 100 miles an hour for the past six months in the war zone and was running on pure adrenalin. It's only last night that I completely let go. I did not realize how tired I was. And Captain, in the future if anyone tells you they do not have to be here, please do not listen to them."

One particular class insisted that when they returned to the US, they would not reenlist. I heard them repeating a joke that they used to tell each other: If they messed up, they'd be sent "to see the guy downstairs in the basement." From that, I deduced that they must have been working with an interrogation unit. That is mentally demanding work that takes a toll on your morality.

Although I think our transition work helped them, I made sure that I alerted the team back in the states to give them additional support (which they did). War is hell, but for some more than others.

Leaders must take responsibility for transitions. In any organization, people are moving to new functions or departments, transferring to new units, being given new responsibility through promotions, joining and departing organizations. Leaders need to make these entrances and exits as smooth and efficient as possible. More than that, they must take the responsibility seriously. Change is a huge challenge, and leaders are in the best position to help their people meet it.

Chapter 12

The Base

My responsibilities in the war zone were varied, requiring me to go to places I'd never been and see sights I'd never seen. I visited a special unit on a Euphrates River dam led by my friend Glen Leverette, a massive infrastructure with a hydroelectric power grid. We traveled there via a V–22 Marine helicopter. After that, I visited Joe Stuyvesant, then the base commander of Al Assad, and while there, we stopped by an oasis. I was told this was the exact spot that Abraham stopped to sleep during his journey recounted in the Bible.

But the issue that occupied much of my time and that I discussed at length with Navy Central Command was whether Kuwait was the best place for our returning warriors.

Danger from Within

In discussion with the Navy chaplain and chief medical officers, we considered moving our facility to Landstuhl Germany or Rota Spain. The latter was an especially attractive site at first glance, but when I flew there and toured the area, I realized there was a problem. In Rota, people had access to alcohol. Our sailors had been alcohol-free for six months to a year. Giving them easy access to alcohol during their transition period was probably not a good idea. Because Kuwait was alcohol-free, it was not an issue there. An additional problem was the law in Spain. If sailors got into trouble, they could be locked up immediately. It would not be good for the sailors or our program if news got out that one of our returning sailors was going to jail instead of going home. After further study, we decided to keep the program in Kuwait.

I've always believed in the value of keeping in great physical shape, and I had a civilian trainer at Kuwait's Camp Arifjan who worked me hard; she called me "Captain Energy." One day I returned home from the gym, my arm hurt, and I figured I must have overworked my left arm biceps. I woke up the next morning and it was worse; it seemed like a small muscle tear on my left arm, and it was also itchy. The next day was even worse, so I went to see the Navy doctor at the expeditionary medical center. They examined it and sent me to downtown Kuwait City for an exam. I ended up getting an MRI.

The result came back within a few days and the doctor said preliminary review showed that it is some type of rare cancer. Initially, I wasn't that concerned, but when I did a search on this type of cancer, the results told me that most people who have it live between three to six months!

That shocked me. As the cliché goes, my life flashed before my eyes. I decided it would be best to go home and be with my wife and family and die there. I thought about funeral arrangements and leaving the family by themselves. I thought about what I should have done or wished I had not done. In the end, I decided I would not have changed anything about the way I had lived my life. My family would miss me, of course, but I was leaving them in good financial shape.

I flew to Newport first and spent two days with my wife and then reported to Walter Reed Hospital for the surgery. Right after the operation, I was still sedated when my detailer Captain Sharpe called to tell me that I was selected for major command. I also got a telephone call from the head Navy Personnel Command, rear admiral Sonny Masso, to congratulate me.

But best of all, the surgeon told me that I had been misdiagnosed and it was not cancer! I immediately made arrangements to fly back to Kuwait and finish my assignment.

Leaders, like everyone else, are vulnerable. Sometimes when you possess great power and influence, when people defer to you, when everyone is depending on you, you forget that you are as vulnerable as the next person. Though I would wish my diagnosis on no one, it reminded me once again of the value of humility. No matter if we're a captain or a chief executive officer (CEO), we are just as susceptible to illness and error as the lowest-ranking person in the organization.

During one of the warrior transitions classes, the chaplain told me that a reporter wanted to participate in the class to understand what we do at the Warrior Transition Program (WTP). She came to see me, and I explained that I couldn't grant her request because people need to be free to express their feelings; that the environment is right for providing spiritual and mental help. The reporter promised me that she would not video any of the sessions or interview anyone. After consulting with my team and my master chiefs, I decided to let her attend. The reward outweighed the risk; there was value in having her communicate what our people had gone through and the sacrifice that our sailors made to protect and defend our Constitution.

I had intended to be there to monitor the reporter, but I needed to travel to Africa to visit our IAs who were there on assignment. I left our team to be with the reporter while I was in Djibouti.

While I was there, though, I received a frantic call from Kuwait. The Army general wanted to see me immediately! The reporter had published an article in which she quoted one of our sailors as saying, "The Army is not taking care of the Navy." I had to do major damage control. I immediately flew back, met in Kuwait with the general about WTP, and explained what we were trying to do. I emphasized that one sailor's comment was not reflective of the entire perspective of the Navy, that most people have a very positive experience with their deployment, and the Army enjoyed working with us. I also had to do damage control back home; the Pentagon had gotten wind of the article. Fortunately, I was able to explain my underlying rationale and they accepted why I had allowed the reporter access. Still, they directed me to allow no more reporters in those classes, though after this experience, I wouldn't have made the same mistake twice. There was no need to even direct me, that is a lesson learned that I entered in my tool bag.

Sometimes, you have the best of intentions and the worst of outcomes. No leader can prevent some situations from going sideways. All you can do in these situations is damage control, and the best way to do is by addressing situations as quickly as you can and as honestly and openly as possible. And of course, you need to learn from what happened and avoid a rerun of a negative scenario.

A Big New Assignment

I received an email from the Navy Personnel Command informing me that I'd be slated for major command. They sent me a list of possible command posts, and one was to be the base commander of the largest Navy base in the entire world, the Norfolk Naval Base in Norfolk, Virginia. I jumped on that, and every day I kept thinking about it, how I would lead it and make it even better. I was excited about the opportunity for an assignment close to home because we had a house in Virginia Beach, which wasn't far from the base.

I said my goodbyes to all the people with whom I had formed close relationships during my year in Kuwait. I returned to Virginia and the doctoral program that I had yet to complete. I had some time before I assumed my new post.

Prior to taking on my new command, an incident occurred that was instructive and inspiring. I was sitting at my desk back at Command Leadership School one day when I suddenly started thinking about a chaplain I had sent on a special assignment. He was a reservist and had gone back to his church and civilian life. For some reason, I decided to get in touch with him, and when

I did, I asked how he was doing. He told me that he had been having problems and needed medical help. He has been going to the Veterans Administration, and they kept giving him the runaround. I told him I'd see what I could do. I immediately called my friend, Admiral Holloway, who oversaw personnel policy N13 for the Navy. When I told him about the situation, he referred me to Navy Safe Harbor Foundation, a group that helps sailors with physical and emotional problems. I called and spoke with the persons in charge, and they made sure that the chaplain would receive the help he needed. I called the chaplain later, and he told me the VA claimed him and set him up for an appointment; he was happy. Looking back, I believe it was a divine inspiration for me to call him out of the blue.

Your responsibility as a leader doesn't end with a given assignment or command. Circumstances may change, but you still need to do what you can for the people who served with you. It is the right and the human thing to do.

Finally, it was time for me to go to Washington, D.C., for a one-year assignment as executive assistant to commander, Navy Installation Command (CNIC) to learn the business before assuming major command.

Learning to Lead a Hybrid Force

During my tour at CNIC, I once represented my boss in one of the CNO Roughead's weekly meetings. It was fascinating to be part of the Navy's highest leadership meeting with the CNO at the head of the table, the vice chief of naval operations (VCNO) that I knew each other back in my Joint Staff days and other top officers. Within a few months, we had a new boss, Vice Admiral Mike Vitale. He came with great energy and a lot of ideas to transform the organization through innovation.

Finally, I was reassigned to be the next CO of Joint Expeditionary Base (JEB), Little Creek-Fort Story. This was part of an armed forces experimental effort on joint basing, and Little Creek would be the only joint base with the Navy leading an Army base. They wanted someone with joint experience who has worked with the various services before to head it. I fit the bill.

During a walk around the Washington Navy yard, a master chief saw me and recognized me as the captain who welcomed him to Kuwait during his IA tour. We caught up for a while, and he made my day when he said he would work for me anytime.

I continued with my doctoral work during this time, and I finally finished all my courses and took my comprehensive exam. I had a week to complete it, and I took time off from work so that I could spend from 7:00 a.m. to midnight each day grappling with the exam's seven tough questions. Around this time, I also joined the Washington, D.C., Scottish Rite (a Masonic order) as a life member to prepare for joining, I spent a weekend at the Library of Congress study room reading about Masonic principles and the responsibilities of this brotherhood.

My very first day in command, part of the base lost power. I would find out that it was a recurring issue. The base has been growing steadily, but the infrastructure upgrade was not keeping up.

Leaders juggle a lot of balls, and they need to become skilled at keeping them moving and up in the air, which is not an easy task when the power is going out and a million other distractions arise.

I set three priorities at the very start of my command priorities that were connected but distinct. Focusing on these issues would help me achieve positive outcomes.

First and foremost, I needed to know my team. These were my base HQ personnel. I had twenty-five department heads to run the base with a total staff of nine hundred. I had to ensure that they had the tools, training, and everything they needed to discharge their duties faithfully daily. I also needed to earn their trust. I told them that my main job was to take care of them while they take care of everybody else. Focus forward, I told them; I've got your back. I structured the weekly department head meeting to enhance relationships between the entire team, keep each other updated, and strengthen the bonds between all team members. I knew I was making progress toward this first priority when people stayed after the meeting to talk and catch up with their colleagues.

My second priority involved the actual base population, the people I was tasked to care for. These were the 155 tenant commands on base. I endeavored to meet every single one of them during my first three months in command. When I told Cynthia Findlater, my executive secretary, she thought this goal was improbable. I told her I needed to do it. I would visit two in the morning and two in the afternoon for an average of thirty minutes per visit. I set an aggressive schedule. I had Cynthia print the biography of each commander with a blurb about each command's mission and review it prior to a visit. When visiting with the commanders in their offices, we would start with small talk designed to help us know each other, and then we'd talk about the command and its challenges, specially those having to do with the base. Next, I would take a tour of the command spaces to see the issues under discussion. Afterward, we would return to the CO office and agree on what support was needed from me. Though I told each CO that their staff should work with my staff to resolve issues, I added a necessary option. If the COs didn't agree with any staff decision, they could meet and discuss the issue personally with me before the final decision. I also said that if I can't do what they're requesting, I would tell them why I could not (usually the reasons had to with policy, laws, or lack of money).

This process ensured that the COs knew that they had direct access to me, their base commander. Sometimes, small things would become big deals if not addressed effectively. For instance, one of my commanders told me that they never knew when the base's back gate was closed. As a result, they had almost been late to an important meeting (they had to go around the entire base to get in). I took note of it and from then on, my base CO permission was required for closing a gate; I would send a personal note to all base leaders and tell them about the gate closing, why, and for how long.

This may not seem like a big deal, but the devil is in the details. Little things like this can irritate people no end and create frustration. Too many small problems like this can affect morale. Therefore, I prioritized addressing these issues.

I wanted to communicate that I cared about the issues my people cared about, and one way I helped send this message was by taking notes when meeting with the base leaders and then have Cynthia file my notes with their bios. Later on, when a base CO called or visited me, I would pull out my book and quickly review their bios and my notes, and I was able to identify the specific issues about which they were concerned and ask if they had been resolved. My tenant COs were always impressed by my "photographic memory" – they were amazed I could remember issues we had discussed months ago during my initial briefing.

My third priority had to do with external organizations off the base. That group included my boss and his staff. I had to attend a weekly meeting where we coordinated region wide issues. Our budget and policies flowed down from Navy region Mid-Atlantic. I also met regularly with our five base captains during this time, having breakfast once a month to facilitate our cooperation. During these breakfasts, I obtained an invaluable overview of their bases, the challenges they faced, and how we might help each other.

I also needed to develop a relationship with the political groups in the area. Specifically, Virginia Beach Mayor Will Sessoms, who was a great fan of the base. He would personally come to all major events on the base with his wife. The City Council was also very engaged with the base, and I made it a point to meet most of the council's members. I also met with the city's chief of police and the fire chief. I met several times with Congressman Scott Rigell, as well as Governor Bob McDonnell. I was also involved with a variety of other outside groups, but one of the most significant groups personally was the Pearl Harbor Survivors Association. It was a very active association with over twenty-five living members, and the president was Mr. Frank Chebatar. Frank was almost 90 years old and would come to the base often to either clean up the memorial there or just drive around, but he would always stop by to see me. He called me "his captain," a title that I accepted with pleasure. Every December 7, we would have the Pearl Harbor remembrance in front of the memorial. I would listen to Frank telling his story on the USS Phelps, a navy destroyer. Frank would weep at times, as he remembered his fallen shipmates on that fateful day.

Leaders have multiple constituencies. To neglect even one of them can be a missed opportunity. To prioritize all of them often provides a path for solving problems.

To resolve the electrical power issue plaguing our base, I made it my number one priority. It finally was sent through official channels for funding but seemed to get lost in the bureaucracy and was eventually taken off the list for funding.

Fortunately, I had developed a good relationship with Mayor Sessoms and told him about the electrical power issue that I had been working on for two years. I explained how one of my Navy Seals said that he had better power in Afghanistan than in the US on my base. Mayor Sessoms called Congressman Scott Rigell and asked him if there was nothing he could do for Little Creek. Not long afterward, the CNO was meeting with Congressman Rigell, who asked him about the status of the Little Creek power issue. The CNO, of course, was taken by surprise. The CNIC admiral himself got in touch with me immediately afterward and asked about the situation. I explained the situation and how it is a well-known problem in Navy circles. During a congressional visit to the region, the main facilities guru for the House Armed Services Committee paid me a visit. He wanted to see the electrical power issue. After he saw it, he agreed that we were eligible for direct congressional emergency money, which fixed the issue for good. I recommended that the small building housing the new power station be named for Congressman Scott Rigell.

To build a team spirit on base, we had various events. Some of them included a quarterly base conference where I briefed all commands and took their questions. I would have most of my key staff accompany me to address any base-wide issues, focusing on policy issues or changes. Our regular communication system was excellent, ensuring that most of the issues were raised and resolved routinely without need of the conference. We also had two band concerts during the summer that everyone on the base and in the community both loved (it was free for everyone). Once, we had the well-known band, Kansas.

Despite having a house in Virginia Beach, I needed to live on base to fully discharge my duties as base commander. Though the Navy base had a base CO house and so did Fort Story, I decided to move out of my house in Virginia Beach to live in the Army base because my main headquarters (HQ) and day-to-day work was at the Navy base; I needed to establish a connection with my Army contingents and that meant living on the Army base.

Favoritism is a difficult label for leaders to shake once it's applied. I knew that because of my long naval service, it would be likely that the Army contingent would see me as favoring the Navy personnel on the base. Before that label became affixed, I moved into a house on the Army base. In that way, I counteracted the belief that I would play favorites.

It wasn't as if I had a lot of spare time while I was in command of the base, but I resolved to finish my doctoral dissertation while I had this position. I had done the three-year doctoral course work and had been forewarned that 50% of people who completed the coursework did not get a final doctoral degree. Doctoral students are granted a total of seven years to finish their dissertation, failing to do the dissertation in this time meant they didn't get their doctorate. I also knew that people who didn't finish their dissertation within three to four years of the exam were much less likely to complete it. On top of this, two of my friends completed their dissertations, making me even more determined to finish my own. I had been working on it from 8:00 p.m. to 10:00 p.m. daily, but it was a challenge. I decided to switch research time to the morning – I would read and write from 06:00 a.m. to 07:00 a.m. before going to work. At times, the juice was still flowing at 7:00 a.m., and I would write for another fifteen minutes. Then I moved my start time back to 5:30 a.m. and then 5:00 a.m. I took a whole week of vacation and read and studied from 05:00 a.m. until midnight every day to kick start the process. I was proud when I accumulated 10 pages, then 20 pages, then 50 pages, and continued to pile up the pages until I was beyond the required minimum of 250 pages. When I'd written 600 pages, the challenge then was to pare it down. My wife was my editor-in-chief. Finally, in October 2012, I was invited to go to Newport for my final dissertation defense. I was granted a Doctorate in Philosophy. The hard work that started in September 2006 finally paid off. My dream since I was at Cornell University to become a PhD had come true.

Education never stops and leaders always learn; I will always search for knowledge and understanding. I cannot overemphasize my belief that knowledge is power, and leaders need to acquire the former consistently and hungrily.

This is the right place to tell you a short anecdote. My oldest son, Javier, had also started his doctoral work at the University of Texas–Austin in music performance. In 2010, we made a bet to encourage each other to finish. We said whoever finished second would pay for a five-course, $200 dinner for two, him and I. As we got to the end, Javier finished his coursework and scheduled his final performance. Soon thereafter, I also finished mine and scheduled my dissertation defense. By coincidence, I defended a week before and received my PhD. Javier successfully completed his final performance and received his doctoral degree a week after I was done. He kept his promise and took me to one of the finest restaurants in Austin, TX, and we had a delicious two-hundred-dollar meal, courtesy of my oldest son.

A base CO, like the CEO of a company, has the opportunity to accomplish a lot. I possessed the decision-making authority to solve problems and take advantage of opportunities. Using this authority wisely is the hallmark of leadership. For instance, the engineering people had designed a new building for the base, and they brought it to me for approval. During my daily tour of the base, though, I noticed that this building's proposed location was isolated from the other buildings. The proposed new building was for SEAL Team 8, and I realized that it would be isolated from all the other interconnected team buildings. More than that, it was separated by a road that would have created access problems because of the compound's gates. I drove around and reassessed my approval of the engineer's design for the building. After returning to my HQ, I asked the engineer to come and see me, and we discussed the possibility of placing the new building inside the current compound. He said it would be possible. I called the Seal group commander, briefed him about my discussions with the engineer and asked him if this revised location was okay with him. It turned out that he was ecstatic. He had assumed, like everyone else, that the only possible location was separated from the other buildings. I asked the engineer for a modified design and then gave it my approval.

It's a challenge for leaders to change their initial positions or decisions. It may seem like it suggests uncertainty rather than the decisiveness for which many leaders strive. As difficult as it may be to revisit and revise decisions, it's sometimes the right thing to do. The most successful leaders can swallow their pride and reverse their decisions when necessary.

Sometimes, too, leaders need to fight for what they believe is right. The Army Morale, Welfare, and Recreation directorate had a great, profitable hotel on base located on the beach. The Army wanted to build it up to an eight-story grand hotel, conference center, and recreation center for the entire US Army to enjoy. But the proposed expansion would intrude on my training ground. The Army's top brass visited and tried to convince me to green light this expansion. Nonetheless, I fought against it very hard, making the case that training and national security would be impacted. Fortunately, we won this fight, and I ended up giving this building to the tenant command for their own special training, and they are using it to this very day.

A Military Mayor

When I'm asked what it's like to be a base commander, I struggle to describe the job to non-military people. Bases are disciplined, self-contained environments – the military equivalent of a small city. We possessed a police force, firefighting, a mall or post exchange/Navy exchange, gas stations, car repair shops, airports and helicopter operation areas, ports, and marinas.

My job as CO was to facilitate the smooth operation of all base facilities. We offered over 100 different services to 155 tenant commands with a base population of 23,000 people. When I was there, we were the largest employer in the city of Virginia Beach. Like many CEOs, my day was filled with meetings. I would attend them on-base or off-base for the city, Navy, various organizations, and conferences. Instead of management by walking around, I favored management by driving around (the base was too big to walk) with the master chief so I could eyeball what was going on. At times, I dropped by to see my various department heads without warning. (I didn't want them to spend time preparing to brief me.) I wanted to stop by, say hello, and show interest in them and their work. These "stop-bys" were unconventional, but they helped me develop trust with my team; they learned that my motivation wasn't to catch them doing something wrong but to build our relationship, and they soon accepted and even enjoyed my visits. During our conversations, I insisted on transparency; I would be honest and open with them, and I expected the same honesty in return.

At the end of the day, I would return to my office, and finish going through my inbox and emails. I'd have my secretary and others leave before me as I did my best thinking quietly after they were all gone.

Being a base commander was a different leadership experience than being the captain of a warship. As base commander, I was in charge of a lot more people and functions than on a Navy ship, and the environment was obviously quite different. It was incredibly valuable for me in that it gave me a chance to acquire new skills and knowledge, like management by driving around and stop-by conversations. The more leaders can broaden their base of experiences, the better able they will be to deal effectively with a wide range of problems and opportunities. Even though it may be difficult to step out of your leadership comfort zone, it's worth crossing that line and acquiring knowledge and learning skills that you never had before.

After a few years, it was time to move on. The Navy tried to give me orders to go to Cornell University as the CO of Reserve Officers' Training Corps (ROTC). I refused these orders. Cornell University had always been my place away from the military and work. It was the place where I did volunteer work and was a regular Cornell University alumnus. I did not want to mix these two different identities. Instead, I preferred to spend my final Navy days as a teacher at the Naval War College in Newport. The Navy told me Newport was 90% manned, and I could go to Army Carlisle or the National Defense University in Washington, D.C.

But this was not where I wanted to finish my career. My detailer offered a compromise: If I was willing to accept an assignment involving arduous duty, then I could write my own ticket. They needed someone to go to Saudi Arabia. I took it!

I was not one to disobey orders, but in this instance, I felt I had earned the right to at least protest an inappropriate assignment. Veteran leaders often possess sufficient wisdom to know which assignments are in the best interests of those they will lead. Even though it may be difficult to turn down a job, it's worth enduring the difficulty if every bone in your body tells you it's wrong. Leaders need to master the art of saying no.

Chapter 13

The Last Commands

B efore assuming my command in Saudi Arabia, I took advantage of a language school we had on base with an Iraqi and a Jordanian instructor assigned to teach me Arabic. I studied an hour each day after work for the last six months as base commander. After I detached from Little-Creek/Fort Story, I contacted the Navy folks in Pensacola responsible for languages and told them about my next assignment. They set me up with Berlitz and assigned me a Moroccan Arabic teacher in the morning and an Egyptian teacher in the afternoon. I was immersing myself in Arabic for over a month about six hours a day.

Next, I went to Wright-Patterson Air Force Base for defense security cooperation school for attachés and professionals going overseas. The purpose was to teach us about cultures and the do's and don'ts in the diplomatic world. I relearned and practiced how to behave in a formal dining setting, how to dress professionally, and reviewed other social skills.

I also called on Mark Vandroff, my weapon officer on the USS Gonzalez. (In 2024, Mark is now CEO of Fincantieri Marinette Marine, building the new Constellation class frigates.) He was then working at Naval Sea Systems Command.

He introduced me to the small boat folks because Saudi Arabia was in process of buying sophisticated small boats.

Saudi Arabia: Boots on the Ground

I flew to Saudi Arabia and immediately started my engagement with the Saudis. I was introduced to all the key leaders of the Navy stationed there, and they really appreciated the fact that I could conduct a small conversation in their language. My most important contact at the Royal Saudi Naval Forces HQ was the officer in charge of overall naval operations, the N-3, Rear Admiral Suleman (whom I have stayed in contact with all those years since). My American boss in country was Major General Thomas P. Harwood, who through his actions, reminded me of my convictions about leadership.

When in command or in a leadership position, everything you do and every word that you pronounce matters. Even the words you don't say and the actions you do not commit have consequences, some intended, some unintended.

Another lesson I learned in Saudi Arabia is the value of putting boots on the ground. Some military officers stay on their bases just like some CEOs stay in their offices, rarely if ever exploring their larger environments. If you're going to be effective in those environments, however, you need to familiarize yourself with them firsthand. The best way to do that is to be present – virtual presence is actual absence.

My team in Saudi Arabia was small but dedicated and professional. I was running a team in Riyadh primarily working acquisition and training programs. One such program was a potential $20-billion-dollar acquisition of ships and helicopters named Saudi Navy Expansion Program (SNEP II). My team and I helped make this ambitious program a reality. I also had a small team in Jeddah and one in Jubail supporting the fleet commanders. A friendship developed with my fellow colonels in country, Thomas "Crimminal" Crimmins, Louis "Dupes" Dupuis, Tom Harraghy, and David

"Dawood" Coggins, who made our weekends a bit more enjoyable even though we were without our families.

While in Saudi Arabia, the US Marine Corps officer, Colonel David "Dawood" Coggins and I heard about the existence of monkeys in the area. We plugged in the GPS coordinates and went on our way. We headed south on Route 65 toward Kharj and eventually found ourselves on a dirt road. The directions had us make a left after a factory, go over the railroad track, continue between the two buildings, and then we hit the dirt road again. The road ended at a telephone tower on top of a mountain. When we got to the top, however, there were no monkeys in sight. The mountain was all dirt and sand, no greenery whatsoever. We wandered around and eventually came upon the monkeys. We advanced toward them and threw a few bananas, and they came closer. Meanwhile, another car arrived, parked a few yards from us and a Saudi family emerged – a man with his two sons. After taking some pictures, the sons approached us. We said, "Salaam alekoum," and the sons echoed our greeting. Then the kids came closer, and they shook our hands, curious about Americans. The father invited us to come out of the car for tea. The conversation led to the grandeur of the mountain and the beauty of the place. Then another car pulled in, and it was his brother and his son. They joined us on the carpet previously laid out by the kids' father and we had tea together. Then a prayer call came from a mosque in the distance. The dad asked us to listen. Then he asked his brother's son to do prayer call, and there was joy as he did so. The 10-year-old son placed his hand on his cheek and start making the call to prayer. In a reverential and prayerful manner, the young boy recited the entire call: "There is no God but God!" He knew every word and we could tell he was very focused on his task. He was facing toward Mecca. When he finished, he rejoined the other boys, his father humbly and sincerely gave quiet praise to Allah and offered his many thanks. It was a short prayer, but we all felt the sanctity of the moment.

It's easy to demonize people you don't know. Leaders can't afford to let their actions be influenced by ignorance. As strangers in a strange land – whether you're a military leader or a business leader running an office in a foreign country – you need to meet the people who are part of your new environment and discover the good, the bad, and the ugly.

My wife joined me in Saudi Arabia, and we had a chance to go to Jordan and visit Petra, Aqaba, the Dead Sea, and Wadi Rum. That got me to think about another boy Nidda and I met in Jordan under a tent at Wadi Rum – the Valley of the Moon and the place where Lawrence of Arabia was supposed to have lived. We stopped at a tent at the foot of a huge rock formation near the ruin where Lawrence supposedly lived. Our tour guide, Nidda, and I were the only people there or so we thought – then we came upon a young man who was under a small tent, seated on a carpet. When he saw us, he got up and offered us Bedouin tea. I sat next to him while our tour guide laid down on the carpet, closed his eyes, and relaxed. Nidda went to look at Lawrence's house nearby, and the young man and I began to talk. I asked him why he was out here in the Wadi Rum alone. He said he was not alone; Allah was with him. Then he started telling me about the quietness and the serenity of the place, and how relaxed he was and how much he enjoyed coming here. He said that this was a place where he could pray to Allah and feel His presence.

This experience combined with others demonstrated how religion and politics were one, an inseparable entity in some countries. The Qur'an is basically Saudi Arabia's constitution. It is a concept that is so different from the Western way of life and thinking with a clear separation of church and state. Understanding how religion and Allah were so tightly woven into the citizens' lives was extremely valuable – I began to understand the motivations of the people in part of the Middle East at a deeper level than I had before.

My brother, Franz, also visited with me in Saudi Arabia and we drove hundreds of miles to Bahrain from Riyadh with nothing but desert on either side of the highway. Saudi Arabia is a beautiful place, especially a place called "The edge of the world," located about an hour drive from Riyadh in the Tuwaiq Mountain range. The view is absolutely spectacular. A four-wheel vehicle was indispensable due to the roughness of the terrain. The area had no gas stations, convenience stores, and cell phone towers – none of the man-made structures and services of civilization. As a result, we felt close to nature. My traveling companions and I got out of our vehicle and walked to the very edge of the cliff. We walked on a dirt path with no side rails; one misstep and we would have tumbled down the cliff to the valley, thousands of feet below. The pure adrenaline of walking the path contributed to the experience. We stayed until sunset when the color of the sun paired with the spectacular clouds, turning the whole vista into an almost divine experience.

A Proud Father Interlude

During this time, my middle son, M. Valentino, went through officer candidate school in Newport. The commander of the training unit (whom I knew) requested me to be the guest speaker for this momentous occasion. I flew from Saudi Arabia and had the privilege to speak to the class and welcome my son as my future relief in the Navy. It was indeed a proud moment.

I recalled the time in 1986 when I was still in the program at VT-10, learning the intricacies of naval aviation, and *Top Gun* came out. My boys loved the movie and it inspired my oldest son, now a classical trombonist and my middle one, who joined the Navy.

Years later, my Navy son happened to be assigned as a team member to the same squadron that flew the actual missions in the *Top Gun* movies. He told me about Tom Cruise and the filming of the movie as I stood with him on the deck of the actual aircraft carrier used in the filming. Recently, my wife and I were guests of JEB base Commander Captain Michael Witherspoon, and we sat next to him and his wife as we watched a screening of *Top Gun Maverick*. It brought back a lot of fun memories and I was proud to see some great Navy flying. It was strange to have Valentino born with the release of the first *Top Gun* movie and then have these later experiences with the second one.

Leadership has many blessings and many privileges. You never know what the future will bring when you begin your leadership journey, but you can be assured that if you do a good job, good things will come your way.

The US Naval War College

I had been in the Navy for almost thirty years, and I wanted to finish my career at the Naval War College in Newport, Rhode Island. It would enable me to pass on my knowledge to the new generation, as well as enjoying a place that I have loved from the start.

The US Naval War College, aside from my tour as captain of the USS Arleigh Burke, was the pinnacle of my career. To be among and part of a group of people in search of knowledge while simultaneously preparing our national security defenders was the ultimate, satisfying leadership experience. I reported for this job soon after returning from Saudi Arabia and was assigned senior housing only five minutes away from the college.

The Naval War College has several schools with different missions. I chose to teach in the school that I had attended, the College of Naval Command and Staff. The curriculum consists of three main sections. The first one, Theater Security Decision Making (TSDM) in the fall trimester, which "educates students on effective decision-making and leadership, focusing primarily on the theater strategic level." The winter trimester is when my preferred course was taught, Strategy and War, which "examines how the overall strategic environment shapes operational choices and outcomes;" this is the course where we studied a different war each week. The Joint Maritime Operations course was taught in the spring trimester, and it "prepares students on critical and creative problem-solving skills that pertain to decision-making and leadership in the maritime domain." The official description of the school is "The US Naval War College (NWC) education provides a framework in which military and civilian leaders gain an understanding of the nature and use of naval strategy and organization through its scholastic programs. The NWC programs are conducted at the graduate level."

In the Leadership program, my first class was in the United States Africa Command (AFRICOM) section, and I was delighted to have three young African officers from Sao Tome y Principe, Gabon, and Tanzania in my seminar who shared their national perspectives with the class. The next quarter, I had three international students from Germany, UAE, Tunisia, and another seminar with officers from France, Panama, and Lithuania. Discussions were frank and open, and we explored the what and how of a leader's action and the why of a decision.

Leaders make decisions that affect the lives of people, organizations, and nations. Understanding why leaders choose a certain course of action versus another helps sharpen our own decision-making skill. Even if they don't take a course in this subject, leaders should assess their own whys and in so doing, grasp their rationales and determine if they're valid or flawed.

Senior housing was right next to the war college buildings. Every afternoon when the weather was nice, all of us would gather in the common area in front of the properties. This was the place where we got to know each other and formed lasting relationships. We would talk about our daily assignments and tasks, our children, our past deployments, and sprinkled more than a few sea stories.

Some leaders are workaholics, and as a result they become one-dimensional — they may be excellent strategists and producers, but they often fail to engage their people. We need to take the time and invest the energy in developing and nurturing human relationships.

Retiring from the Military

When it was time to make arrangement for my military retirement, I chose my old boss retired Vice Admiral Dan Holloway to be my guest speaker. For this special event, my oldest son, Javier, composed a special musical piece for trombone that he performed for the audience. He received standing ovation. Then my middle son, Lieutenant Commander M. Valentino Stuppard, memorized the poem "The Watch" and gave an outstanding rendition of it. We celebrated that evening at the Newport Officer's Club. Then in October of 2015, I moved out of housing and transitioned back to civilian life.

When I was at the Naval War College, away from military operating forces, I was able to focus on my transition to civilian life. I met with Cornell University's Simon Krieger, a VP at AT&T who had become a partner at Luciano group, in New Jersey. He referred me to Tom McNeil of MDL Partners and Tom asked me to come up to Boston for a visit. I soon signed up for his seminars and became a client of his. He assigned me a mentor – a senior executive and former CEO, Dr. Bob Gough. Bob's wise counsel helped me to think like an executive. I learned that making the transition to this civilian form of leadership was about a state of mind and what you know. Bob helped me discover potential and strength I did not even know that I had.

My first post-military job was vice president at AECOM for defense affairs in the Middle East. I was reassigned to the Middle East, and while in Saudi Arabia, I continued to learn Arabic and hired Mohd Awad, then working at the Saudi Minister of Defense, to continue teaching me Arabic. Every Thursday, he would come to my compound and we would only communicate in Arabic. In this assignment, my primary job was to support various Middle East ministries of defense in evaluating their defense needs and link them with our appropriate AECOM experts to provide them with workable solutions.

Leadership in the private sector is similar to leadership in the military. In the military, I held myself responsible for my actions and all projects given to me. It was my job to keep my bosses updated by putting myself in their shoes. I employed these same principles at AECOM, and they helped me perform at a high level.

My next job arrived courtesy of a friend in Washington, D.C., Retired Rear Admiral Tony Watson. During my original job search at MDL Partners, I flew to D.C. and discussed my qualifications and what I was interested in with Tony. Tony is one of the Centennial Seven, comprising the only African Americans to command a nuclear submarine in the twentieth century. I first met Tony at a National Naval Officers Association (NNOA) conference in San Diego when he held the position of commandant of midshipmen at the Naval Academy. I was impressed with his demeanor, air of confidence, and savoir faire. He was one of these officers that I wanted to be like when I grew up.

When Tony called and asked me what I was up to, I said I had finished my assignment in the Middle East and was taking a break. He then told me about a new opportunity in Washington, D.C. Tony was the vice chairman of a startup company, The Constellation Blue Group under the umbrella of The Bluestone Group, with a potential $8 billion project in West Africa to build a seaport, an airport, and roads infrastructure. They were looking for a COO and he suggested this might be a good fit for me. I drove to D.C. and met with their team.

I had dinner with CEO Roger Blunt and his wife, Vivian, at the Cosmos Club in D.C. We did not talk about work. Instead, I discussed my time in the military, what I valued, and my years at Cornell University. It was a get-to-know-you meeting. The next day, I reported to the company HQ on M-Street and went right into their morning meeting. I followed their briefs closely and tried to understand their strategy and the status of the projects on which they were working. At a certain point of the brief, the CEO asked me what I would do in this situation. I responded with the action I would take but added that I would look at the situation in an alternative way, just in case the chosen strategy did not work. The CEO nodded his head. Upon completion of the brief, Tony showed me the office spaces, and I met the rest of the team. I then drove back to Virginia Beach. A few days later, I called the CEO to see what he had decided. He asked me when I could start.

I rented an apartment in Washington, D.C. and commuted to
Virginia Beach on weekends. I found a place literally next door to
the office. From my apartment window on the twelfth floor, I
could see my desk in the next building on the sixth floor. I jumped
right into work and continued to develop the plan for a vast project called "L'Épine Dorsale" or "The Backbone," created by
founding chairman of Petrolin group in Switzerland, Mr. Samuel
Dossou-Aworet.

It was a good time for me to be in Washington, D.C. My
youngest son, Charles, had graduated from college with degrees in
mathematics and chemistry and had been working as the statisti-
cian for the state of Texas, in Austin. His job was to work with
various agencies, mostly the FBI, to track crime rate. He was tired
of his job, though, and I convinced him to explore life in D.C. He
got a job in D.C. with the agency that develops and reviews math
questions for various scholastic tests like the ACT and SAT. He
would later meet his wife, Taja, settle in Washington, D.C., and give
us two wonderful grandsons, Ezra and Noah.

My first time meeting with Mr. Dossou was during our trip to
Cotonou, Benin. He flew in from Switzerland to share his vision
about L'Épine Dorsale. We drove with him to the town of Parakou
to see the massive work already started by building a dry port to
facilitate the transfer of goods from the seaport of Cotonou to
nearby countries. This same line of work took me to South Africa,
Nigeria, and Ethiopia, representing Mr. Dossou in various ports
and infrastructure conferences and symposia. Our head project
engineer, C. John Klein was the best in his field. We went to most
of the trips together as I handled project management, and he cov-
ered the engineering perspective.

While in Benin, we went to visit a place called "The Gate of
No Return." On the way there, the guide told us about the slave
trade in Benin and how tribes would capture enemy tribes and sell
them to Portuguese traders. We saw the trading market and walked
along the same route they followed toward the ship that would
take them to the new world. One tree was of particular

importance. The slave traders instructed the captured prisoners to go seven times around this special tree. Apparently, this ritual was designed to erase their origins and history from their minds. We finally arrived at the "gate." CEO Roger Blunt, our Security Chief Marcus Aurelius Hunter, and Chief Engineer C. John Klein, and I toured the place and asked questions. Finally, I called the team to take a picture. Roger opened both arms in front of the gate with his back towards the ocean – Roger proclaimed, "We have returned!" The guide took the picture. I quickly noticed that John was not in the picture. He was on the side looking at us with a sorrowful face and moist eyes. I called John to join us in the picture, and he said he was not worthy to join us. I went to John, gave him a hug, and said, "Everything is okay – we are brothers." He said, "Yes, we are." He joined us and we all took a picture together. Roger, Marcus, and I are Black, and John is White. I had long realized that people are people, and most of us are good people. Most of the different ways we view ourselves or others are man-made, whether it be race, religion, sports teams, and so on. I have come to accept people for who they are and not by the groups with which they associate themselves.

I spent over a year working on this project. I learned much about the economy of Africa overall, mainly focusing on West Africa. The project slowed down as we waited for the final go or no go – it seemed like it would be months before we knew if the project was going to happen.

My work with The Bluestone Group taught me the value of a small team. In the Navy, I led a lot of large teams. Leading a smaller group is different. We performed well because we were agile and able to respond to taskers on a dime. In a small team, everyone counts. It is crucial to surround yourself with people whom you can trust and who can understand your vision and able to carry it forward.

While I was waiting to see if this project received a go-ahead, John O'Callaghan, a friend who had gone through the same executive course with me at MDL Partners gave me a call. He told me he was working for this great company, Bambu Global, in Boston comprised of several researchers and PhDs who had worked at Polaroid, including their chief scientist. I flew to Boston to meet the team and found their work to be fascinating. They had over sixty patents and a dozen more pending. They were looking for someone who knew enough about science and engineering to understand on what they were working. In addition, they wanted someone who understood the military acquisition system and how it worked and had been operational with the military as well as who could make a match based on their many patents.

They invited me out to dinner, and I met the Vice Chair Satish Agrawal, COO Saleem Miyan, and three other vice presidents. It was not an interview; it was only dinner. During dinner, we talked about the company, my career, and my management philosophy. We agreed to meet the next day at the company headquarters in Lowell, Massachusetts.

After a tour of the company, they showed me a few of the patents and projects on which they were working. A week later, Saleem called me to set up a start date. Soon afterward, I moved out of my apartment in Washington, D.C. and moved to Lowell.

As usual, I worked very hard to learn what I needed to do a good job. In this case, it was learning about all their patents; I chose six with significant military applications. I presented one technology to the US Air Force Research Lab at Wright Patterson Air Force Base. The Air Force invited me to New York City to present it. In the first ever US Air Force Pitch Day, which was designed like the show, *Shark Tank*, I advocated for our unique technology and was instantly awarded a Phase I contract to develop it further. I presented another significant technology to Navy Systems Command (NAVSEA), which could revolutionize a certain aspect of stealth technology. I piqued their interest, and they asked me for additional briefings. I also started working with Huntington Ingalls Industries on a technology for our newest submarine, SSN-X, which would improve human performance and endurance using light spectrum.

I was enjoying this work, when in March 2020, the company placed my startup, Canopy Defense, on hold temporarily to focus all Bambu Global company energy on finding a way to detect COVID. We originally thought COVID would only last a few months. Unfortunately, it took much longer than anticipated.

This is when I founded my own small consulting firm, CLS Consulting & Leadership Services. I wanted to devote the company to leadership development using all my years of training and education. My first client was DMS International under the leadership of Magdalah Silva and Daniel Silva. My primary role was to be a liaison for them and their clients like the Navy, NASA, and the Department of Energy. My small veterans-owned company was doing well when I received a call from my old shipmate from the Navy, retired Commander Elaine Luria. She ran and won her first race to serve as congresswoman of Virginia's Second District, consisting of coastal Virginia, which included Hampton Roads.

When I was captain of the USS Arleigh Burke, Lieutenant Luria was married to Lieutenant Robert Blondin, my operations officer. Elaine was also serving her tour as Ops officer as well on another destroyer. As you may remember, from my time there, I used to have a monthly wardroom get-together at my house for all officers and their significant others to cement the relationships on the ship. As such, Elaine would be present as much as her Navy schedule allowed.

When she called, she told me that her First District director was moving out of the area and she would be delighted if I could be his replacement. I told her I would get back with her after consulting with Nidda. Nidda said, "You cannot possibly say no to a dear friend like Elaine, would you?" I said, "Of course not." I called Elaine and we settled on a day for me to start a new adventure.

Working as a congressional staffer and district director, I worked long hours at a job that was quite different from any of the ones I held previously. Elaine was very detail-oriented, and she would even read the footnotes I wrote and commented on them. I would not expect any less from a nuclear trained officer! Elaine cared deeply about the district. Most people think their congressperson is on vacation when not in session in Washington, D.C. – not so for Elaine. This is actually when my work doubled. She would have days packed with events, meeting people, and trying to provide solutions to their issues.

During COVID, I would get calls from North Carolina, Massachusetts, and New Jersey from folks asking me to help them with issues because people from other states heard that we actually answered our telephone and helped people. I told them I could put them in touch with my counterparts in their own states. I had marching orders for the eight folks I supervised (covering a constituency of over 700,000 people): To answer the phone and do our best to address all issues brought to us. At times, if it was an urgent matter, I would follow up to ensure the issue was properly resolved. Most of the people I spoke with were astounded that I would call to follow up on them. Again, that is what I would have done as a base commander or a Navy ship captain – why would I not do the same for the people that I was sworn to defend?

Not all the callers were respectful, and some were just plain rude or mean. I told my people that if the caller was not polite, they should come and get me and I would speak with that person. I found out some folks refused to accept any logical answers we gave them. Their mind was already made up – it was only their way or the highway.

Leaders in government, the private sector, or the military are all highly effective when they follow bedrock principles: Work hard, respect others, follow up on raised issues, be flexible, and defend your beliefs clearly and convincingly. They learn to earn trust through their daily interactions with people; if people trust you, they will come searching for you when they need someone in a position of authority. At the same time, as President Abraham Lincoln once stated, leaders cannot please all the people, all the time. You have to strive to do your best with a clear conscience.

After this stint with Congress, I went back to my consulting firm and worked with IMS Gear in Virginia Beach under Guenter Weissenseel, one of the finest company presidents I have ever known. Guenter embraces traditional leadership principles symbolized by warm handshakes and eye-to-eye contact. Once, Guenter's team of accountants and lawyers were negotiating the final design and construction phase along with the cost for his current headquarters and manufacturing plant. They came to an impasse and both sides refused to budge. Guenter and Tim, the CEO of the construction company, asked everyone to leave the room and come back in half an hour. Guenter and Tim talked it over, came to an understanding, looked at each other in the eyes, and sealed the deal with a handshake. The building was constructed on time, within budget, and to the highest standard. Today, years later, Guenter and Tim go to each other's company parties and they are great friends. That is an example of a win-win cooperation, where no one is trying to take advantage of another. Guenter walks around the company and people look forward to speaking with him; he knows everyone by their first name.

During a talk with the provost of Old Dominion University (ODU), I explained the leadership development and training progression of Navy COs. He told me he had four new deans starting at the university the following semester. I agreed to write a case study for ODU's Academic Affairs Leadership Team (AALT) orientation for Fall 2022. Attendance originally was for the new deans, and by the time we were done with the case study and ready for presentation, we decided to add several vice presidents, the two vice provosts, and several other deans. The retreat was well received. Later feedback from the new deans made it clear that it was very useful and facilitated their transition as new deans.

Old dogs can and should learn new tricks. These high-level academics were veteran leaders, but they were open to acquiring new knowledge and skills. People who are professionals with a lot of experience may have achieved a lot, but it is never too late to learn something new or a new way to look at certain issues.

Finally, in August 2023, Colonel Thomas Crimmins (with whom I had worked in Saudi Arabia and had been promoted to major general) was assigned to be commandant of Joint Forces

Staff College (JFSC) in Norfolk, Virginia. JFSC was founded by President Eisenhower after World War II. It was established as the Armed Forces Staff College in 1946, which was its name when I attended back in 1999. It became part of the National Defense University in 1981, with a primary mission to "Educate national security professionals to plan and execute operational-level joint, multinational, and interagency operations and instill a primary commitment to joint, multinational, and interagency teamwork, attitudes, and perspectives."

Major General Crimmins was looking for a dean of administration and had interviewed several candidates for the position. Although, I had not seen him since I left Saudi Arabia, we had remained in contact. During a lunch meeting, Crimmins told me about the position and recommended that I apply for the position, if interested – which I was, and I did apply. I followed the same interview protocol as every other candidate. After a few weeks of waiting, I received a call that my background and experience fit the position for which they were looking.

This is my current assignment (as of this writing), and I love every minute of it. A few weeks ago, I was also assigned to serve as dean of students as well. The best part of the day is in the morning; as I go to work, and pass a plaque marking the exact spot that Admiral Arleigh Burke, as CNO, broke ground for the building that I enter every workday.

Chapter 14

A Sea Dog's
Final Lessons

L ooking back, my biggest leadership challenge was not about leading others. It was about leading myself and fighting against self-doubt. I immigrated to the United States at the age of nineteen, starting behind those who were born in this country and spoke English. My accent caused listeners to doubt my words. I suppose the assumption was that if you can't speak English perfectly, you can't understand it as well as you should. I remember vividly, on my first ship, when I was designated to give officer training about engineering propulsion. I explained it using the Navier-Stokes equation, describing the motion of viscous fluid. My shipmates were flabbergasted that I even knew this concept. After the training, several of them congratulated me on the caliber of the training; they obviously weren't expecting me to grasp the concepts. It was not an issue of my knowledge or experience, but the skepticism conveyed by the chief engineer and the captain. They were not confident initially that I could run the ship's engineering plant underway. I had to convince them by the quality of my work.

In the best of circumstances, it's tough to be a good leader, and these were not the best of circumstances. I had to convince myself as well as others of my competence.

My other biggest leadership challenge was on the USS Arleigh Burke after observing how the wardroom was separated by groups. New leaders who are called upon to heal existing divisions among their people face a high degree of difficulty. As you'll recall, I came up with unconventional ways to unite them, including the share-a-story strategy at meals. The vision I had for the way I wanted the ship to operate depended on a unified corps of officers. I achieved that vision, and the unified philosophy continued long after I left the ship.

If I regret anything as a leader, it's that it was difficult to maintain a work-life balance. The level at which I needed to operate required every ounce of energy I had. I would come home physically and mentally exhausted. During my time in Hawaii, especially, I was doing the job two levels above my current rank, requiring that I would leave the house by 5:30 a.m. and return well into the evening.

Fortunately, this work-life imbalance was managed effectively by my wife. In 2025, I celebrate forty years of marriage. I have three formidable sons (Javier, Valentino, and Charles), and four awesome grandsons (Jace, Korbin, Ezra, and Noah). When people congratulate me for the success of my sons, I give the credit to my wife. She was the one to read books to them and watch *Sesame Street* with them. She limited their TV time to one hour each, even on weekends. She made sure that our sons had boundaries and her attention. Though I tried to contribute to parenting them as much as I could, I was away a lot. When my youngest son Charles was born, I left on deployment one month later and came back after six months. When I returned, I picked Charles up and his confused expression communicated, "... and who would you be?" Leaders have many different and effective leadership styles, and mine was what experts call "servant leadership." My belief was: I am here to serve my team, my family, and my country. I worked hard to have my team focus forward and excel knowing that I had their back. For people to completely devote themselves to the mission and let you have their back, trust must be fully established and tested. Trust is an absolute element in this style of leadership. My first task in command was to build this trust, ensuring that people understood that "I do what I say, and I say what I do." I did not want any say-do gaps or surprises. I inherited this style from my father and mother who devoted their life to serving the people of Haiti – one worked tenaciously to save their souls and the other to provide for their education as a teacher. They modeled serving others as the ultimate path to happiness.

This style of leadership fits my personality and my personal beliefs. In the hierarchic system of the military where discipline is key to survival, my style was unusual. It required a balance. The team knew that my primary job was to support them and get them what they needed to complete the mission assigned. Yet, at the same time, no one ever doubted who was running the show.

During my deployment with the NATO ship captains, we had developed a superb team as we patrolled the Mediterranean. One of the captains (not from the US) told me that I was an unusual US Navy captain. He explained that other captains were a bit more arrogant, in large part because they possessed sophisticated weapons and systems. He noted that though I, too, was in charge of a ship with these weapons and systems, I lacked pretention. I explained that individuality is important in the US and in the Navy, that we are allowed to have our own personality. I added that we didn't have a cookie-cutter leadership style that we had to follow. This freedom gave our captains a military advantage, I added. The enemy could never predict what we might do in battle, because we all had different ways of implementing strategy.

The freedom I was granted suited me; it enabled me to be an authentic leader. My leadership style reflected exactly what I was thinking, who I was, and who I still am.

I'm an advocate of granting others the flexibility to find and use their authentic style.

Leaders should not be forced to be someone they're not. They should also be encouraged to adapt their style to situations and to use tools that fit a particular set of problems or opportunities.

It doesn't matter what a given person's leadership style is – authoritative, transactional, or coaching-oriented. Leaders must understand each style and the associated tradeoffs. In servant leadership, mission accomplishment is primary and equal to the welfare of the team. The main difference from the other styles is the power relationship between the leader and the team. In a servant leadership construct, the primary focus is on the team and not the leader. The leader is an integral part of the team. Everyone knows their role and positions and everyone executes the mission to the best of their abilities. The final credit belongs to everyone.

Time is a great teacher, especially about leadership. Though my leadership style didn't change radically over time, it did evolve based on my experiences. In fact, I never saw myself as a leader when I was younger. I just tried my best to meet the expectations of my parents and the challenges set for me by my older brother, Franz. In sixth grade, Franz promised me if I achieved a certain GPA, he would give me a bicycle. I did not believe that I could but gave it a shot. To my surprise, I exceeded the GPA goal. It showed me that if I set a goal for myself, I might just make it – a good lesson for a leader. My Korean Tae Kwon Do teacher motivated me to teach classes, and at Cornell University, when I founded my own club, I was leading the club. At Fairchild Republic Company, I was elected president of the Young Engineers' Society; not because I lobbied to get the position but because it seemed right to everyone in the group that I take the position. I was only one of them, serving as their liaison to top leadership. I always had what was best for them in my mind and never saw myself as their leader.

In fact, I didn't join the Navy to become the captain of a ship or a leader of any kind. In fact, my opportunity was open to all. Any citizen could go to college, join the US Navy, and become an officer. Yet, people have different aspirations. I happened to become an officer because I wanted to design airplanes for the Navy. Upon becoming a division officer, I saw my job as caring for my division, ensuring they have what they need to do their job. Again, I saw myself as serving their needs, while taking care of myself as well. I was the conduit between my division and the bigger Navy, the system. I understood the system and could use my knowledge to benefit my team.

Somewhere during my training and education, I read that a good officer lightens his bosses' load. I tried to do that. I would look at the project, a problem, or an issue from the perspective of my superior officers. I would then try to present them with solutions, courses of action to choose from, instead of bringing them problems to solve for me. I would analyze the situations, come up with my own way to resolve them, and then compare my bosses' solutions to mine. I would see which approach was better. At times, their ideas won out when I realized I'd been viewing an issue only from my perspective, and when I saw it through their eyes, I recognized what I was missing; or I saw how their fervent belief in their solution might carry the day; or I deferred to their greater experience.

And sometimes, their solutions were a complete mystery to me. Regardless, I formed strong ideas about leadership based on working with my various bosses over the years. I determined that the best leaders care about their people and always have the welfare of the crew in mind as they make decisions. I also learned that some leaders would make great decisions but their decision-making process was wrapped up in their egos.

All this had an effect on my leadership thinking, but the effect on my leadership style was slow and incremental. One change that was more noticeable involved my discussion with a base commander in San Diego that I recounted earlier. His one regret was that he was too soft and people did not execute his orders when he needed them to and he did not push it hard enough. Instead, he waited for them to execute on their own schedule. He recommended that I be hard at first and ease up as time went by.

I took this lesson to heart and used it when I reported to Hawaii on the USS Reeves; to my surprise, it worked. I was a hard-ass at first and did not let anyone mess with me. Then as time went by, I loosened up and people responded positively. Eventually, I mastered the hard-soft art of leadership.

By the time I retired from the Navy, I had formed my own leadership beliefs. The essence of great leadership is to believe in yourself, be loving with those you are charged to lead, and be respectful to all you encounter. As I internalized these principles, I found myself making decisions that accomplished the missions assigned and caring for my team simultaneously. It was not an either-or choice.

The leadership lessons contained in this book are particularly relevant today for the military, government, and private industry. Leaders in all sectors need to get their people to be more productive, and they need to do so with kindness and caring. Remember my mantra: Do good, be good.

I also hope students who are just starting on their leadership journey take the lessons of this book to heart. My story is one of a young immigrant who grew up poor, in a country labeled as the poorest in the western hemisphere, who came to the US and realized the American Dream. It shows that regardless of where you were born, regardless of your status and lot in life, there is always hope. We can all aspire to be successful leaders.

You may not be able to think about tomorrow, you may not be able to predict from where your next meal is coming, but do not give up. Leaders persevere.

Throughout the book, I included leadership lessons drawn from a wide variety of experiences, extrapolating each learning from a specific challenge or opportunity. Here, I will provide more overarching lessons gleaned from my entire journey, ones that have emerged after reflecting on all these experiences. I hope they will guide you on your journey of leadership, wherever it may take you.

- Give thanks for the little things.

Without the little things, there would be no big things. I remember September 10, 2001, a day like any other in the Pentagon, an ordinary early fall day. The next day changed everything. I lost friends in the terrorist attack. Memories that remain are the seemingly insignificant moments we had together, maybe going out for a cold beverage or a meal somewhere in a foreign port.

Be grateful for the small victories of leadership. Leaders express gratitude; it's a humanizing action, and it's the right thing to do. Thanking people for their assistance on a project, for their effort and for their kind words has two benefits. First, it acknowledges the person and reassures that individual that you are aware of what they've said or done. Second, expressions of gratitude provide the opportunity to publicly give credit to the universe – to God or to any higher power in which you believe. It helps leaders recognize their own relative insignificance in relation to the universe. Third, giving thanks reminds you that you need to pay it forward – that your actions in the future should be such that others will want to thank you for your words and deeds.

- Appreciate life and what you have.

Leaders who are resentful and envious of others are never comfortable in their own skin, and their people sense this discomfort. We can always complain about what we do not have. Take satisfaction from what you've achieved. Each passing day is gone and will never come back. Take time to relish everything – your promotions, your successes, your ability to mentor and lead. People who are satisfied with what they have are in a much better position to help others.

- Develop perspective.

Someone always has it worse than you, just as someone has it better. It all depends on your perspective. In any life, multiple actions are unfolding at the same time. Your mood is dependent on what action is occurring. If your team fails to achieve its mission, you probably feel down in that moment. If your team achieves its mission, you probably feel up. Recognizing that things change based on what's taking place in a given moment in time will help you find perspective. Leaders need perspective to avoid becoming unrealistically high or low. Perspective determines how you understand an action and how respond to it. You're likely to make better decisions with a good perspective.

- Have a vision.

Everything is mental before becoming physical. It all starts in our mind. A nation without a vision perishes, and it is the same for businesses too. Leaders need to know and understand where they want to go in order to create or discover the path.

- Take care of yourself and your people.

As captain of a ship, I learned that if you take care of the people who report to you, they will take care of the ship and of each other. You can't lead like Captain Bligh of the HMS Bounty, whose crew famously mutinied. Yes, there are leaders who are dictators, but they will never complete their missions at 100%.

- Keep yourself fit – physically and mentally.

If the captain is sick or mentally unfit, then the ship suffers. To take care of others, you have to be fit – go to the gym, exercise! In terms of cognitive fitness, develop and lead by principles. Be true to these principles and disregard naysayers. Leaders must find ways to handle distractions and detractors and protect their direct reports from interference. They need to stand firm and believe in themselves and their missions. This mental strength helps leaders stay the course.

- And one more time, let me urge you to follow my mantra: Do good, be good.

Index